THE IMPORTANCE OF

Chaucer

John H. Fisher

SOUTHERN ILLINOIS UNIVERSITY PRESS

CARBONDALE AND EDWARDSVILLE

Copyright © 1992 by the Board of Trustees,
Southern Illinois University
All rights reserved
Printed in the United States of America
Edited by Julie Riley Bush
Designed by Joanna Hill
Production supervised by Joanna Hill

95 94 93 92   4 3 2 1

Library of Congress Cataloging-in-Publication Data

Fisher, John H.
The importance of Chaucer / John H. Fisher.
p.   cm.
Includes bibliographical references and index.
1. Chaucer, Geoffrey, d. 1400–Criticism and interpretation.
2. English philology—Middle English, 1100–1500.   I. Title.
PR1924.F57   1992
821'.1—dc20   91-12626
                                                                      CIP
ISBN 0-8093-1741-9

Excerpts from "Troylus and Criseyde," "Canterbury Tales," "Book of the Duchess,"
"House of Fame," and "Legend of Good Women" from *Complete Poetry and Prose of
Geoffrey Chaucer,* 2d edition by John Fisher, copyright © 1989 by Holt, Rinehart and
Winston, Inc., reprinted by permission of the publisher.

Excerpts from Sir John Fortescue, *De Laudibus Legum Anglie,* ed. and trans. S. B.
Chrimes (Cambridge UP, 1942), reprinted by permission of the publisher.

The paper used in this publication meets the minimum requirements of American
National Standard for Information Sciences—Permanence of Paper for Printed Library
Materials, ANSI Z39.48-1984. ∞

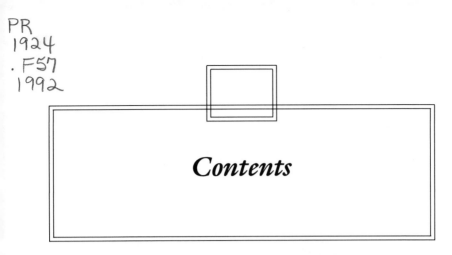

Contents

Preface

There are very few people who read and write English who have not heard of Geoffrey Chaucer, and most of them have read—perhaps even in Middle English—the General Prologue to the *Canterbury Tales* and a tale or two like the Miller's bawdy fabliau or the Nun's Priest's beast fable about Chauntecleer and Pertelote. Most college students who go further in the humanities take a course in Chaucer, and learn about him, along with Shakespeare and Milton, as one of the "fathers of English literature." Behind the study of this triumvirate lurks an awareness of their "importance." But importance in what sense? Nearly all discussion is of their art and their oeuvre. Their importance is assumed but seldom defined.

In this book I explore Chaucer's importance as a cultural cynosure. As the first important secular writer in England, as the first influential writer in the English language, as the first English writer to broaden the subject matter of literature beyond the court and the cloister, he was germinal not only to the development of the English language but to the development of our view of the subjects that literature can treat, and to our view of authorship. His influence cannot be understood simply through explication of his poetry. As the "new historicism" is reiterating (after two generations of "new criticism" which denied it), an artist's achievement grows out of domestic, political, and intellectual ambiance which needs to be examined if we are to understand the reasons for its impact.

Many materials exist for the study of writers' ambiances after about 1600—diaries, letters, and contemporary commentary of all sorts. But such materials are very scarce for medieval writers, and especially scarce for writers in England, with the result that most discussion of Chaucer has focused almost exclusively on the text. I have ventured in this book to go beyond the text. In so doing, I am being unscholarly, since the soundest scholarship is that which is based on the firmest evidence. But there are aspects of how Chaucer's domestic life, education, and audience must have influenced what and how he wrote that have been slighted simply because we have so little firm evidence. Paul Strohm in *Social Chaucer* (Harvard University Press, 1989) comes closest to setting him in his social context, but even he has refrained from drawing conclusions about the effect of this context upon Chaucer's performance and influence.

In this book I have undertaken to infer from what little evidence we do have, as well as from the text, in an effort to understand how Chaucer's achievement was shaped and why it has had such a profound impact upon his successors. I have attempted throughout my discussion scrupulously to distinguish between facts and inferences. But I have based my interpretation upon the inferences. That is what the book is about.

The three inferences that most disturb conventional views are those that relate to Chaucer's domestic life, to his possible experience in the inns of chancery and inns of court, and to the possibility that Henry V and the Lancastrian government sought deliberately to promote his poems as models of what could be accomplished in the vernacular. Russell Krauss's documentation of Thomas Speght's suggestion (1598) that Thomas Chaucer was not the son of Geoffrey has never been kindly received.[1] But Krauss's evidence is hard to refute, and my inference that possible disdain for Chaucer's domestic situation may have been taken to justify disdain for the English patois of which he was such an exemplar might help to explain why we have no manuscripts of Chaucer's poems written during his lifetime. I have not tried to reargue the evidence. The materials are readily accessible and readers must make up their own minds about the inference.

The idea that Chaucer was educated in the inns of court also goes back to Speght.[2] This view was generally accepted through the time of Manly and Rickert. It was first called seriously into question by D.S. Bland, and subsequently by S.E. Thorne and E.W. Ives. Bland's objection is strictly methodological:

> The Inns of Court themselves must be considered to be products of the early fourteenth century, though direct evidence is slight. But whether they also provided at that time [i.e., in the mid-fourteenth century] the extra-legal education which Fortesque says they provided in the mid-fifteenth century is a question which cannot be answered with certainty. . . . [It is] a matter that cannot be decided without positive evidence from the period in question.[3]

Again, I have not reargued the evidence. The question seems to be one of whether the inns of court provided formal legal education. Tout long ago set this question to rest.[4] Legal training in the common law (as contrasted with university training in canon law) was a form of apprenticeship like most other guild training. Lawyers into our own century could be trained by "reading law" as apprentices to established lawyers. No one argues that the inns of chancery and of court were not in existence when Chaucer was a young man, and I am content to rest upon the generalization in the 1980 edition of *The Oxford Companion to Law* that the inns of court are "voluntary, unincorporated societies which have existed in London from very ancient times (at least the thirteenth century) in which originally apprentices-at-law lived a semi-collegiate life, subject to a common discipline and government, and pursuing a common system of education and, after call to the Bar, of professional life."[5] There is no reason in the world why Chaucer could not have been an early participant in this form of education, whose effect upon his subject matter and style can be so clearly discerned.

The inference about the Lancastrian promotion of Chaucer's poetry rests in turn upon the inference that Henry V deliberately promoted the adoption of the vernacular. Most histories of the English language still seem to imply that standard English just happened, but I am sufficiently a disciple of Thomas Kuhn's *The Structure of Scientific Revolution* to believe that most technical and cultural developments can be traced to innovation by one individual.[6] I have elsewhere assembled the evidence that Modern Standard English came into existence between 1417 and 1422 in the English Signet letters of Henry V.[7] The present inference is that Henry's switch in 1417 to writing to his chancellor and the English cities in English was not precipitous, but the outgrowth of many years of thought and discussion. Part of this process of gestation could have been Henry's encouragement of his cousin (or uncle) Thomas Chaucer to assemble Thomas's father's (or stepfather's) foul papers and produce the first fair copies of Chaucer's poems as models of cultivated English.[8] This would place the allusions by Hoccleve and Lydgate to their "master" Chaucer in a more specific light. No doubt they admired his artistry, but if his poetry were considered to carry with it a ukase, we could better understand the particular nature of the fifteenth- and sixteenth-century tributes to Chaucer as the creator of and criterion for cultivated English. This remains an inference, as does the part played by Henry V in the adoption of English by government and the guilds, but the coincidence of dates and people with the appearance of the first secular manuscripts in English produces a fascinating scenario which I sketch out in the last chapter.

We know so little about the biographies of Chaucer and his contemporaries and the social setting in the fourteenth century that any discussion that goes behind the text is bound to be speculative. A scholarly monograph would address itself to the ambiguities in and the many possible interpretations of the data. That is not here my intention.

What I have tried to do is, while acknowledging the lack of specific information, to show that certain assumptions about Chaucer's life and ambiance help to fill out the picture of how he became the cynosure he is for all of those who write in English and read its literature.

I wish to thank Mark Allen, David Fowler, and Jan White for reading portions of the manuscript and Henry Kelly for informative discussions. All have saved me from grevious errors, although none of them, I am sure, subscribes to all my heresies. I thank Holt, Rinehart and Winston for permission to quote Chaucer's text from J. H. Fisher, ed., *The Complete Poetry and Prose of Geoffrey Chaucer,* 2d ed., 1989, and Cambridge University Press for permission to quote S. B. Chrimes's translation of chapters 48–49 of Sir John Fortescue's *De Laudibis Legum Anglie,* 1942.

Abbreviations

The Importance of Chaucer

1.

Chaucer and the Emergence of English

It is hard today, when English has become an international language, to imagine when it was the disdained patois of an occupied island. The courage it took for Chaucer to write poetry in English for a French-speaking court might be comparable to Tennyson's writing in cockney for Queen Victoria, or Robert Frost's writing in Appalachian for John Kennedy's inauguration. The success of Chaucer's experiment was gradual, not immediate, and its process is a fascinating glimpse into cultural history. We have ample evidence that his writing was admired by his contemporaries, but we have equal evidence that it was received gingerly. As far as we know, not a bit of it was copied or distributed until after his death. So it appears that the reemergence of English in the fourteenth century was a complicated affair.

It was complicated not only because French had been the language of power and culture in England since the Norman Conquest, but also because French itself, along with all of the other European vernaculars, was in the process of emerging from the domination of Latin. Latin had been for some fifteen hundred years throughout Europe the language of administration, commerce, law, religion, learning, and literature.[1] Imperial Latin, which we today call classical Latin, had been the administrative language of the imperial civil service of Rome and its provinces. Julius Caesar, in commencing the Roman Empire, provided the model for what became imperial Latin in his correspondence, and especially in

his periodic reports on his victories in Gaul. His successor, Augustus
Caesar, centralized the administration of the expanding empire by creating an obedient civil service, and it was the paperwork of these imperial
"notaries" that standarized the language and disseminated it throughout
Europe.[2] Most of the classical writers whom we think of today as
"authors" were, like Chaucer himself, actually members of this civil
service. Julius Caesar we have mentioned. Cicero was an aedile, a praetor,
and a consul. Tacitus was a consul; Pliny was an imperial high commis-
sioner; Horace, Strabo, and Seneca were notaries. Poets like Virgil,
Ovid, and Juvenal were dropouts. They were trained for the civil service
but chose instead to devote their lives exclusively to literature.

The extent to which government and commerce slipped back into
orality during the decay of the the imperial administration in the sixth
and seventh centuries is a moot question.[3] It appears that the Germanic
tribesmen were slow to learn to write. But we know that Theoderic,
who formed the Ostrogothic Kingdom in Italy (493–526), preserved
some aspects of the writing-based Roman administration through
agents like Boethius, who had been trained in the imperial civil service.
And the Roman Church, which at once assumed the mantle of the
Empire, carried its administration on in the forms and language of the
Empire. As the pope assumed the role of the emperor, so the papal curia
(*curia* is Latin for "court") assumed the role of the imperial civil service.
The great missionary effort inaugurated by Pope Gregory (540–604)
disseminated what then came to be called church Latin rather than
imperial Latin throughout Europe. The struggle over the next five
hundred years to assert the supremacy of the pope over emperors and
local kings and bishops identified spiritual and political power with the
language of the papal curia. When Charlemagne revived writing-based
secular administration in the eighth century, it was with the language
and forms of the curia.

Throughout the Roman Empire and until the time of Charlemagne,
the attitude towards spoken dialects was like our attitude towards spoken
dialects today, only more so: that Standard Latin was the only possible

language for formal communication. Charlemagne was the first ruler to recognize that Latin was not sufficient when at the Council of Frankfurt (794) he stated (the record is, or course, preserved in Latin; we don't know what language Charlemagne actually spoke!): "No one believes that God should be worshipped in only three languages [Latin, Greek, and Hebrew]. God is worshipped and man's prayers are heard, when his demands are just, in any language." And shortly after Charlemagne's death the Council of Tours (823) ordered priests to translate their sermons into *rusticam romanum aut theotiscan* (Vulgar Latin or tribal dialects; "theod" means "tribe").[4]

In spite of this recognition of the vernacular dialects that became the Romance and Germanic languages, Latin continued as the language of administration and learning until the Renaissance, and in some cases into the present century. The situation of the Roman Church is familiar. Only in the last decade has it begun to relinquish Latin as its exclusive language both for worship and administration. The secretariats of medieval governments were known as chancelleries (in England "chancellery" was reduced to "chancery").[5] The chancel is the enclosed space around the choir of a church where the priest ("priest" is the Anglo-Saxon term for Latin *clericus*) said the divine service seven times a day. But when he was not saying the divine service, the "clerk" was available to do "clerical" work for his master. In this he employed the *ars dictaminis,* the art of dictation,[6] as the Roman notaries had done and as secretaries do today (though less and less thanks to dictating machines and word processors).

But during the Dark Ages the role of the secretary was much more influential. Most "executives" then were illiterate barbarian warlords like Theoderic the Goth or Charlemagne or even King Alfred. After about 500, any writing-based administration (at first very little, but more and more as time went on) was initiated by the "dictator" instructing the clerk in his native tongue, be it Gothic or Frankish or Anglo-Saxon. The clerk then wrote the missive in Latin, and it was transmitted to the recipient whose clerk read it to the "auditor" in *his* native tongue. Writing was regarded like mathematics today, an international system

of symbols for written communication not associated with the colloquial. For nearly a thousand years, writing was Latin and Latin was
writing. The story of the Renaissance is the gradual movement of secular
administration, commerce, and learning away from clerical monopoly
into the hands of executives who could read and write their own missives
and contracts in their own languages.

The movement towards vernacular literacy was faster in Italy (eleventh century), Spain (twelfth century), and France (thirteenth century)
than it was in England (fourteenth century) and Germany (fifteenth
century).[7] The tenth-century commencement in England under King
Alfred was aborted by the Norman Conquest; the eleventh-century
commencement in Provence was aborted by the Albigensian Crusade.
Vernacular literacy affected religion first, then commerce and administration, and last of all the world of learning. Until World War I, some
professors in European universities still lectured in Latin; until World
War II, doctoral candidates at the Sorbonne had to write a dissertation
in Latin; until the 1960s Latin was an entrance requirement at select
colleges; and the International Union of Botanists still requires specifi-
cations for new species to be set forth in Latin as well as in the native
language of the discoverer.

Religion in the Middle Ages occupied a curious middle ground.
The language of the Church was Latin, but the laity to whom it minis-
tered did not know Latin. So both vocational and avocational materials
addressed to the clergy were in Latin, but some of the earliest writings
in all the vernaculars were religious instruction and entertainment addressed to lay people. Virtually everything written in vernacular until
after the sixteenth century—including Chaucer's—was written by someone whose only education in reading and writing had been in Latin. It
was accepted (as it is accepted today about third-world languages and
vulgate dialects) that the vernaculars could not express the abstractions
and subtleties of Latin. Indeed, we have to wait for Richard Hooker
and Francis Bacon after 1600 to see English used as eruditely as Latin
was used by such twelfth-century Englishmen as John of Salisbury and

Walter Map. Chaucer and his contemporaries began the transmutation of the profundity and eloquence of Latin into English.

But Chaucer's eloquence did not come directly from Latin. One of the reasons for the tardiness of the emergence of literature in English in comparison with French, Spanish, and Italian was the Norman Conquest. From 1066 until after 1350 England was trilingual, with the ruling class speaking in French and writing in Latin, while the populace continued to speak English.[8] During the Anglo-Norman period, from 1066 until 1204, the kings of England were the dukes of Normandy and they and their barons spent more time looking after their estates in France than their estates in England. In the agrarian feudal economy all institutions of power, culture, and learning were in the hands of the secular and ecclesiastical aristocracy whose spoken language was French and whose written language was Latin. Whatever middle class existed was composed of retainers to the aristocracy. This complicated the linguistic situation in England because Latin and French were undergoing the same developments in France that Latin and English were to undergo in England. As in England, a religious literature emerged in French addressed to those who did not know Latin. But after the twelfth century, as a bureaucratic and commercial middle class began to arise throughout Europe, more sophisticated literature in the vernacular began to be written in France (the troubadour poets in Provence, Chrétien de Troyes, the *Roman de la Rose*), in Italy (Dante), and Spain (*El Cid*) emulating the eloquence of the Latin classics. But during this period, the English court and emerging middle class continued to speak Norman-French. This delayed the emergence of literature in English nearly a hundred years—Jean de Meun finished the *Roman de la Rose* about 1277 and Chaucer finished *Book of the Duchess* in 1368.

In 1204 King John Lackland lost Normandy but was able to maintain control of southern France, which was no more eager than England to be under the domination of Paris. It is important to distinguish between the English connections with Normandy and with Aquitaine. In Normandy, the Anglo-Norman aristocracy were hereditary barons who owned fiefs of their own. In Aquitaine the English king was overlord, collecting rents from the local French barons. The English (Anglo-Norman) aristocracy in general owned no fiefs of their own. For the next 250 years the kings of England tried to regain their lands in Normandy and hold on to their other French possessions, sometimes, as under Edward III and Henry V, with apparent promise of success.

However, after 1204 the English aristocracy no longer possessed estates in Normandy and could no longer think of themselves as French dukes and barons. As they came, perforce, to think of themselves as English, the language spoken by the majority of the population began to seep upward from the populace to the court. But this was a gradual process that involved as much assimilating as displacing French. The process was at its most crucial stage from 1350 to 1400, during Chaucer's lifetime. Until the end of the fourteenth century, the language and culture of prestige in England remained French.

This was the great era of French influence in the Middle Ages. The geographical centrality of France, the wealth and population its fertile lands generated in an agricultural economy, its supremacy in chivalry (fighting on horseback—originally "chivalry" had meant simply riding horseback) when a knight in armor was equivalent to a modern tank, made France the superpower of the continent, but superpower in the medieval tribal sense. Until long after Chaucer's death there was no unified France, but a kaleidoscope of competing dukedoms of which the English were merely the most disruptive. French nationalism is not considered to have emerged until Joan of Arc (c. 1430). But even though most of the energy of France during this period of cultural ascendancy was spent on internal conflict, enough was left to spill over onto all its neighbors.

In 1309 when the pope and his curia moved to Avignon, France became the center of religious as well as of secular supremacy. Its modes and codes of combat, religion, literature, dress, food, and manners set the standard everywhere, especially in England, which had for so long been an integral part of France. With the successes of Edward III the

English court became for a while the criterion of French culture. After the battle of Crécy (1346) it enjoyed enormous prosperity in booty and ransoms. Edward III became the model of a chivalric king.[9] His tournaments were the showcases for martial skills and lavish entertainment for knights from all over Europe. Chaucer described such a tournament in the Knight's Tale in the *Canterbury Tales,* and the friend whose French poetry he translated, Sir Oton de Graunson, achieved international fame at such events. The number of tournaments that Edward sponsored is incredible. For example, he is said to have sponsored nineteen in the eight months between October 1347 and May 1348. This would mean something like two a month, of affairs that lasted a week or two each. His creation of the Order of the Garter to recognize the outstanding warriors of Crécy—both English and French—created a vogue for chivalric honor societies that other rulers emulated. After the battle of Poitiers in 1356, the kings of both France and Scotland, along with many of their distinguished barons, were maintained in elaborate courts near Windsor while they awaited ransom. Most of the participants in the tournaments and courts were themselves from France and were served by scores if not hundreds of French retainers. Froissart served as secretary to Queen Philippa from 1361 until her death in 1369, and while in England he began collecting materials for *Les chroniques de France, d'Engleterre, et de pais voisons,* a chronicle of the Hundred Years War between the English and French.

Below this international aristocratic stratum, however, the English commonality were beginning to assert their own culture. It was English-speaking longbowmen who had cut down the French chivalry at Crécy and Poitiers. An argument used in the English Parliament in 1295, 1344, 1346, and 1376 to raise money for the wars was that French victory would annihilate the English language.[10] In 1362 the clerks admitted for the first time that Parliament was addressed in English, and in the same year Parliament decreed that all legal proceedings had to be conducted in English because the litigants could not understand French. (As a matter of fact, this statute was not enforced, and the common law courts continued to plead in French till 1731, but that is another story.) It seems that by the 1360s, most oral exchange in commerce and government was carried on in English, although the records were still kept in French and Latin. Edward seemed sensitive to the growing chauvinism of the populace when he selected English mottos for his tournaments, like "It is as it is," and "Syker as ye wodebynd" ("Trustworthy as the honeysuckle"). His only French motto was for the famous Garter tournament of 1349, "Hony soit q' mal y pense" ("Shame on him who thinks evil"), which was evidently intended especially to impress the continental chivalry.

Richard II is a prime example of the interweaving of French and English.[11] He was known as Richard of Bordeaux because he was born in 1367 in the elaborate court the Black Prince maintained at Bordeaux after Edward created him Duke of Aquitaine. Throughout his life, Richard was so Francophile that he would not pursue the war with France, to the distress of his chivalry. He was French in his dress, food, and culture. He had not a single English title in his considerable library. Yet there is evidence that his first language may have been English. One of the most notable events in his otherwise unhappy reign was his English address to the hostile peasants in the Peasants Revolt on 14 June 1381 at Mile End (just outside Aldgate, where Chaucer could have been looking on). Evidently he liked to read in English, too, for about 1386 he commanded Chaucer's friend John Gower, whose previous poems had been in French and Latin, to write the *Confessio Amantis* in English "that he himself it mihte loke / After the forme of my wrytynge" ("that he himself might look at it in the form that I wrote it"). His predilection for English was sufficiently known for Froissart to observe when he presented Richard a copy of his *Chroniques* in 1394, "The kynge was gladde and loked in it, and reed yt in many places, for he coulde speke and rede French very well."[12]

Henry V, who came to the throne in 1413, was the king who began formally to transform English government from French to English, which made possible the eventual standardizing of English spelling and grammar.[13] Henry's official correspondence was in French from his accession in 1413 until his second invasion of France, but on 22 August 1417, from his French castle of Touque, he addressed his first signet letter of instruction in English to his lord chancellor, and from that time until he died in 1422, all of his official correspondence was in English. We have no explanation for this move. People before the Renaissance were exasperatingly silent about their motives. But Henry's motive must have been political, like Edward III's when he chose English mottos for his tournaments.

Henry's letters were to secure money and supplies from Parliament and the corporations of London and other English cities, and addressing them in English was obviously expedient. A few letters in Henry's hand are preserved and the spelling and syntax of his 105 signet letters is so similar, even though they are in the hands of at least thirteen different scribes, that they must have been modeled on Henry's own usage. The spelling and syntax of these letters was adopted by the clerks in other offices of chancery (as the government bureaucracy was called), then by clerks of the guilds and the Corporation of London, and the scriveners and independent clerks. The chancery clerks and stationers were the ones who contracted to copy most of the manuscripts of Chaucer, Gower, Lydgate, Hoccleve, and other literary writings that have been preserved. Their "Chancery Standard," as it came to be called, was by the middle of the fifteenth century the more-or-less uniform language for all government and business in England, and set the model for William Caxton's printing.

Caxton, until he was forty-eight, had been an important official in the Company of Mercers in London and Bruges, carrying on his business in French and Chancery Standard.[14] So we may say that Standard English as it emerged in the sixteenth century is the reflection of the personal style of King Henry V modulated through the practice of government bureaucracy, the London scribes, and the early printers.

But Henry and chancery provided only the authority and the mechanism for making English official. It was writers in the generation before Henry V who had begun creating the Franglais that we now call Standard English. Under the influence of King Alfred (849–899), Old English (or Anglo-Saxon) had been standardized as a highly inflected Germanic dialect and adopted earlier than anywhere else in Europe as a national language. That is a story in itself. But the Anglo-Saxon Standard was confined to the court and monasteries in Wessex, in the southwestern part of England that remained under English domination after the Danish invasions. Beginning in 797 the north of England had been gradually overrun by the Danish Vikings. By 870, they had taken East Anglia, London, and Canterbury, and were poised to overrun Wessex as well. Alfred's great achievement was to defeat them and sign the Treaty of Wedmore in 886, which preserved the Kingdom of Wessex with Winchester as its capital.

By 1066, the conservative, inflected language that we find in the Old English classics like *Beowulf* (we call the language Anglo-Saxon, but the culture Old English) was not the spoken language of the majority of the English population. In the two-thirds of the country that fell under the Danelaw, a patois of English and Scandinavian dialects developed, full of Scandinavian words, and, more importantly, almost totally lacking the Germanic inflections and grammatical genders. This is the process known to linguists as "pidginization," in which inflections disappear and communication is confined to substantive words.[15] The Norman Conquest eliminated Anglo-Saxon as the language of culture, replacing it with Latin and Norman French. But from 900 to 1400 (and indeed throughout most of rural England and lowland Scotland today) ordinary people spoke, and speak, varieties of the English-Danish patois. Aelfric, Wulfstan, and the latest entries in the Anglo-Saxon Chronicle before 1066 preserved the Anglo-Saxon grammatical forms. But by 1100 the inflections began to disappear from the entries in the Chronicle. Clearly what the Norman Conquest extinguished was an Anglo-Saxon literary tradition that no longer represented the language of the majority of the common people. And when English began to be written down again after 1200, it was in the uninflected, ungendered form of the common speech.

English writing from 1066 to Henry V was all in local dialects, like missionary translations of the Bible into the local dialects of illiterate communities today. These dialects were not uniform in pronunciation, spelling, grammar, or vocabulary.[16] This was the situation in Chaucer's time. The three principal poets of the fourteenth century—Chaucer, Langland, and the *Pearl* poet—wrote in three totally different dialects: Chaucer in the dialect of upper-class London, the *Pearl* poet in the dialect of Lancashire, and Langland in a south midland melange. Will, the Dreamer, locates himself in the Malvern Hills in Worcestershire, but the author evidently lived in lower-class London. We find Chaucer the easiest to understand and call him the father of Modern English because he wrote in the dialect of the London court which would, in the next generation, after Henry V, become the prestigious form of English for government and business. But we should understand that Chaucer did not "create" the language in which he wrote. It was being created by the intermingled French and English business class emerging in London at the end of the fourteenth century.

Chaucer's own biography exemplifies the nature of the society out of which the standard language arose.[17] The surname we know him by is French, derived from French *chaussier,* "shoe-maker"; his grandfather, known as Robert le Chaucer, Robert Malin le Chaucer, or Robert of Ipswich, first lived in London on Cordwainer Street—*cordwain* being the Anglo-French form of "cordovan," from Cordova, the home of fine Spanish leather. We do not know why Robert was called "the shoe-maker" or why he lived on "shoemaker street," because his father in Ipswich (the poet's great-grandfather) was known as Andrew de Din-nington (presumably a place name) or Andrew le Taverner (another trade name), and Robert was known in London as a vintner, as was his son John Chaucer, the poet's father. The poet's grandmother, Mary, was married three times, to a pepperer and two vintners, and both of her sons, John Chaucer and Thomas Heron, were vintners.

John Chaucer's home that Geoffrey grew up in was on Thames Street, in the parish of St. Martin's in the Vintry. One might suppose that a family that had lived for several generations in Ipswich and London used English as its domestic language, but who can say? Vintners were wholesale wine merchants; the source of their merchandise was the English possessions in the south of France, especially Bordeaux, and their market was mainly the French-speaking court. John Chaucer became involved early with the court. In an age when warfare was still the principal occupation of the aristocracy, anyone hoping to do business with the gentry was practically required to have military experience. We may recall how important military service has been for American candidates for political office. Since people in the fourteenth century were often recorded under different names, we cannot be positive about identity, but a John Chaucer is listed in a campaign against the Scots in 1327, when the poet's father would have been about seventeen, about the age at which Geoffrey himself went on a campaign in 1359. And, more importantly, a John Chaucer was granted letters of protection to go to France in the king's service in connection with the opening campaign of the Hundred Years' War in 1338. In his later career, John Chaucer exported wheat and wool from Ipswich and served as collector of customs in Southampton and other ports, the sort of office his son Geoffrey held in London for twelve years. John Chaucer must have been very prosperous. Wine was the most important commodity imported into England, ninety to a hundred thousand tuns a year, two thousand tuns for the king's household alone. The king's exchequer received an import tax on each tun, from which, along with the export tax on wool (the two taxes collected by John Chaucer and his son Geoffrey), it supported the royal household, the national bureaucracy, and military adventures. In his dealings both as merchant and government official, John Chaucer moved in a society in which French was still the language of power and prestige, even though English may have been his domestic language.

Young Geoffrey must have grown up in a multilingual society. We have no documentary evidence as to his elementary education.[18] All schools were under the control of the Church, so he probably went to elementary and grammar school at St. Paul's Cathedral, less than a five minutes' walk from his home on Thames Street. St. Paul's had a select choir school for eight small boys, probably not unlike that in the Prioress's Tale in the *Canterbury Tales,* where the "litel clergeoun [diminutive of "clerk"] seven yeer of age . . . sat in the scole at his prymer" (lines 503, 517), and listened to the older students recite in Latin, which he could not understand. The "primer" was the first schoolbook, containing the ABC's, Lord's Prayer, Ten Commandments, psalms, and hymns, all in Latin. The first primer not in Latin that we know of was William Marshall's of 1534, *The Prymer in English, with certeyn prayers and godly meditations, very necessary for all people that understande not the Latyne Tongue.* But presumably all primers in Chaucer's time were still in Latin. However, the situation for Chaucer would have been even more complicated. At the end of the *Polychronicon* (c. 1327), Ranulph Higden had complained:

> This apayrynge [impairing] of the burthe tongue is bycause of tweie thinges; oon is for children in scole ayenst the usage and manere of alle othere naciouns beeth compelled for to leve their owne langage, and for to construe their lessouns and their thynges in Frensche, and so they haveth since the Normans come first to Engelond. Also gentil men's children beeth i-taught to speke Frensche from the tyme thet they beeth i-rokked in their cradel, and can speke and playe with a child's broche [trinket]; and uplondisshe [rural] men will likne hym self [make themselve like] to gentil men, and fondeth with greet besynesse [take great care] for to speke Frensce, for to be i-tolde of [respected].

Higden wrote in Latin. This passage is modernized from John Trevisa's 1385 translation of the *Polychronicon.* And Trevisa adds a comment that has been frequently misunderstood:

> This manere was moche i-used to fore [before] the firste moreyn [plague, 1349] and is sithe [since] sumdel i-chaunged; for John Cornwaile, a maister of grammer, chaunged the lore [learning] in gramer scole and construccioun [analysis] of [from] Frensche in to Englische;

and Richard Pencrich lerned that manere techynge of hym and othere men of Pencrich; so that now, the yere of oure Lorde a thowsand thre hundred and foure score and fyve, and of the secound kyng Richard after the conquest nyne, in alle the gramere scoles of Engelond, children leveth Frensche and construeth and lerneth on Englische.[19]

This has sometimes been taken to mean that by 1385 children were being taught English in school, but that is not what it says. It says that before 1349, all *recitation* was in French, and that John Cornwall introduced a change in *recitation* from French to English. The reading and writing being taught was still Latin and was to continue to be Latin into the eighteenth century.[20] Sir Philip Sidney wrote that it is "a peece of the Tower of Babilons curse that a man should be put to schoole to learn his mother tongue."[21]

St. Paul's choir school had a remarkable library of more than a hundred books, some thirty mostly on science and law donated by its headmaster William de Tolleshunt in 1328, and eighty-four mostly of classical poetry donated by its headmaster William de Ravenstone in 1358 (presumably they would have been there when Chaucer was a student, c. 1348–1356). Ravenstone's books were remarkable. At a time when Winchester College had only one classic in its library, Virgil's *Aeneid,* and Merton College only two, Seneca and Boethius, Ravenstone's will listed Claudian, Lucan, Juvenal, Statius, Horace, Virgil, Ovid's *Metamorphoses,* which Chaucer called his "owene book" (*House of Fame* 712), and other classics, and Tolleshunt's will listed books on civil law and the natural sciences. Neither will listed many religious books, which made up the bulk of most medieval libraries. Ravenstone's will indicates that the books could be borrowed. So if Chaucer was as precocious as we imagine he must have been, we know where he began to read the books he referred to throughout his life. He would have stayed in the choir school till his voice broke (age twelve or thirteen), and crossed the yard to grammar school until he joined the household of the Countess of Ulster (age fourteen or fifteen).

So Chaucer's earliest education was in Latin, construed in French, with hardly any attention at all to English. He had to receive some instruction in French because the Anglo-Norman dialect, which in 1066 had been equal in prestige to Parisian, had by 1350 become provincial. This is the point to the observation about the Prioress's French in the General Prologue to the *Canterbury Tales:* "Frenssh she spak ful faire and fetisly [elegantly], / After the scole of Stratford atte Bowe, / For Frenssh of Parys was to hire unknowe" (l.124–26). The spoken language of the Bourbon court and the written language of its *chancellerie royale* in Paris had by 1350 become standard; all the French court poets except Froissart wrote in Parisian dialect. Froissart's continuing to write in the dialect of his native Hainault (in modern Belgium) may betray consciousness of his English audience and of the growing overtones of nationalism associated with the French of Paris.

The next formal stage in Chaucer's education, when he was about fourteen, was service in the household of Elizabeth, Countess of Ulster, the wife of Prince Lionel, second son of Edward III. The first documentary evidence about Chaucer is the fragments of the household accounts of the countess from 1356 to 1359 which name "Galfrido Chaucer" and "Philippa Pan" among her most constant attendants. John Chaucer's influence is evident in this appointment, because it was then, as it would still be today, very unusual for a commoner to become an attendant in a royal household. At puberty there were three avenues open to a middle-class boy: an apprenticeship to a master in one of the guilds leading to a commercial career, holy orders and the university leading to a career in the church or "clerical" work (since most of the administration both of church and state was still done by clerics; we recall the Clerk in the General Prologue who "hadde geten hym yet no benefice [ecclesiastical position], / Ne was so worldly for to have office [commercial position]" [l.290–91]), or service in a courtly household that could lead to military reputation, knighthood, and perhaps even marriage to a wealthy heiress. Geoffrey obviously chose the last, although in a few years—by 1360—he opted out and turned to a new avenue just then opening up: the inns of court and the national bureaucracy.

During the three or four years he served in the household of the Countess Elizabeth, Chaucer would have become immersed in the French chivalric culture for which the court circle of Edward III had become exemplary. The idea of courtesy (etymologically "courtliness," "courtly behavior") was the most important contribution of French culture to the medieval ethos. This ideal, memorialized in the "Trouthe and honour, fredom and curteisie" of Chaucer's Knight (*CT* 1.46), originally had little to do with the sentimental dalliance and drawing room manners we associate with courtesy today. It represented rather an exacting code of conduct for a soldier, either lay or religious. The terms by which Chaucer characterized the Knight have narrower, more specific meanings than they do today: truth was troth, fidelity; honor was reputation; freedom was generosity; courtesy was decorum. This ideal is explored in a widespread genre of propaedeutic "courtesy" literature directed to both religious and secular audiences, beginning with the Bible, spreading to epics like *Beowulf,* instructive tracts like *Ancrene Riwle,* and courtesy books and poems.[22]

How romantic love became a matrix in which the courtesy ideal developed has preoccupied scholars over the years.[23] Chivalry per se is a military code; the chivalric codes in Persian, Arabic, and Japanese literature have little to do with *eros* in any form. But from the troubadours onward, as Jonathan Nicholls observes, courtesy most frequently denotes a system of behavior and ideal values fostered by courtly love.[24] At the beginning of this century Henry Adams, in *Mont-Saint-Michel and Chartres* (1904), presented the cult of love as a deliberate program fostered by the Church and by women to tame the barbarian warrior. Denis de Rougemont, in *Love in the Western World* (1940), interpreted romantic love as a Freudian obverse to professional killing. *Eros* ought to signify continuity as *thanatos* signifies termination; but a cult of sterile romantic love is the worship of death in another form. More recently Erich Köhler has interpreted courtly love as transposed feudal service. The lady is an icon that enables the lover to contemplate and come to terms with the impotence of his feudal situation. The lady is a metaphor for the lord; the lover is a metaphor for the courtier. The language of courtly poetry is a sublimation that helped poets (who were themselves feudal retainers) to cope with their subjugation in the real world.[25]

This transference, which may have been unconscious in twelfth-century troubadour poetry, had become a conscious manner of saying one thing and meaning another in allegorical love poetry from the *Roman de la Rose* onward. Laura Kendrick has shown that the hundreds of love poems by Eustache Deschamps, which so contrast with the antifeminism of his *Miroir de mariage,* are really addressed to his male patrons, on the one hand pleading for their favor, on the other hand admonishing himself to keep a leash on his emotions and "animal" instincts.[26] Dante and Petrarch likewise employed love poetry as a manner of saying one thing and meaning another. The transference is sometimes hard to accept. Malory's *Morte d'Arthur,* enshrined as a testimonial to chivalry and romance, was described by Roger Ascham, tutor to Elizabeth I, as "open mans slaughter and bold bawdrye,"[27] and Froissart's assertion that his *Chroniques* record "the honourable enterprises, noble adventures, and deeds of arms performed in the wars between England and France"[28] strike the modern reader as whitewash over little more than pillage and rape.

The joining of chivalry and love led in the twelfth century to the creation of a cult of love parallel to the cults of Christianity and feudalism.[29] The figure of the God of Love sitting enthroned attended by Youth, Beauty, Lust, and the other personifications of courtly love was parallel to God surrounded by his saints, the pope surrounded by his curia, or the king surrounded by his courtiers. The Court of Love, first popularized by *Roman de la Rose,* was an allegory of power, accessible only to the select. As it reappeared in so many French court poems, and the poems of Chaucer and Gower, the Court of Love became an allegorical representation of the behavior and sophistication that distinguished gentle from vulgar society.

How conscious Chaucer may have been of the multilayered meanings of the cult of love is, as we shall see in the last chapter, one of the principal concerns of recent Chaucer criticism, and we will return in later chapters to the ways in which Chaucer transmuted the language and sentiments of French chivalric poetry. The important point to make in this chapter is that his principal contribution was to find English idiom to express the depth and sophistication of the French courtly tradition. French poetry was as much the literature of the aristocracy in England as in France, and its vision of love as a cultural marker had begun to be expressed in the English adaptations of the French romances like *Sir Perceval of Galles* and *Gawain and the Green Knight*.[30] Classical literature, the basis of all formal education, likewise had much to say about morals and manners. Chaucer was the first English poet to meld the sentiments of courtly love with easy and frequent allusion to classical authors, to philosophy and theology, to astronomy and astrology, to rhetoric and genres of literature. Such enrichment is a commentary on the audience as well as on the author. Only a sophisticated audience could have appreciated the virtuosity of Chaucer's achievement. From the French court poets, Chaucer learned that writing about love was a way of treating power and emotions; from the Italians, he was soon to learn more about synthesizing chivalric idealism with Latin humanism. But more of that in good time. His education in Elizabeth's household marked the beginning of his melding of learning with love.

In addition to knowledge of courtly culture and courtly literature, Chaucer evidently acquired his wife in the countess's household, which may provide further evidence about his domestic language. The other attendant most frequently mentioned in the Countess of Ulster's records is Philippa Pan, and in 1366 a Philippa Chaucer was granted a life annuity of ten marks by the king for her service as *domicella* to Queen Philippa. Although we cannot be sure the Philippas are the same, it appears that the page Geoffrey married the damoiselle Philippa, and that the "Pan" stands for "Panneto," one of the forms of the name of Sir Paon de Roet. The sixteenth-century herald Robert Glover identified Chaucer's wife as the daughter of Sir Paon and sister of Katherine Swynford, mistress and in 1396 wife of John of Gaunt, and mother of his son John, Earl of

Somerset, from whom Henry VII was eventually descended. Gaunt's son by Blanche of Lancaster, Henry Bolingbroke, founded the house of Lancaster; the descendant of Gaunt's son by Katherine founded the house of Tudor. Chaucer was closely related by marriage to the center of hereditary English power.

Sir Paon de Roet had come to England from Hainault in the entourage of Queen Philippa when she married Edward III in 1327. On his tomb in St. Paul's, he is identified as "Guyenne Rex Armorum," King of Arms of Guienne, meaning that he was in charge of recording the genealogies of the noble families in England's valuable territories in Aquitaine, an important office since genealogy would govern inheritance of land and titles. Given its continental associations, Sir Paon's household probably spoke French, and that may well have been the language of whatever household Geoffrey and Philippa established.

While we are about it, we should go ahead and discuss the inferences about the marriage. That Philippa was of gentle birth, the daughter of a knight in the queen's household, and was granted her annuity without any reference to her husband a year before Geoffrey was granted his suggests that Geoffrey married above himself and that Philippa's position helped his career. But there is the indirect possibility that it was a marriage of convenience.

One of the great mysteries of Chaucer's biography is the parentage of Thomas Chaucer,[31] who in the early 1390s married a wealthy heiress, Maud Bergersh, whose daughter Alice married the Duke of Suffolk, whose grandson married the sister of Edward IV, and whose great-grandson John, Earl of Lincoln, was declared heir apparent to Richard III but was put aside when Henry Tudor won at Bosworth Field. In stratified English society, it is not usual for the descendants of an esquire of lesser degree to move so far. Thomas followed Geoffrey in renting the Westminster house and in holding similar administrative appointments. But after using Geoffrey's seal and coat of arms for a few years, he designed his own seal and shifted to the de Roet arms, and there is a rumor dating as far back as Speght that Geoffrey was not Thomas's father. Modern scholars have suggested that he was the illegitimate son of John of Gaunt, which would account for the annuities and gifts that Gaunt lavished upon the Chaucers, particularly on Philippa, throughout her life. In particular, it would explain why she was admitted in 1386 to the confraternity of Lincoln Cathedral in a Lancastrian ceremony that included Gaunt's son Henry Bolingbroke, but did not include her husband, Geoffrey. The confraternity had been established by the Bergersh family into which Thomas Chaucer married a few years later. Such parentage would account for the advancement of Thomas and his family. In 1389 Thomas was retained for life to serve in John of Gaunt's household, and his career is marked by grants and commissions from Gaunt and the monarchy. He was sheriff of Oxfordshire and Berkshire, and constable of Wallingford Castle. He was the King's Butler to Richard, and Henry IV, V, and VI, an office that carried responsibility not only for the wine of the royal household, but also for the collection of Petty Customs, the tax on wine imports that was so important to the support of the government—an office resembling that of Geoffrey Chaucer and his father, John. He was a member of Parliament and several times Speaker of the House of Commons.

Gaunt's long liaison with and eventual marriage to Philippa's sister Katherine and the advancement of his Beaufort children by her are well known, and those who resist the suggestion of a relationship between Gaunt and Philippa wonder why the parentage of Thomas would have been kept secret when the parentage of the Beauforts was so public. But it could have been the very publicity of the parentage of the Beauforts that made it impossible for Gaunt to acknowledge Thomas. Philippa and Katherine as sisters were, according to canon law, in the first degree of affinity, and marrying (or having sexual intercourse with, since the laws of consanguinity apply whether the union is formal or informal) both of them while both were still alive would render them and their offspring "infamous" in the legal sense, that is, forbidden the rites of the Church.[32] This may account for the fact that contemporaries were so vague about Thomas's parentage. For example, when Lydgate, who extolled Chaucer as his "master dear," wrote a poem around 1416, *At the Departyng of Thomas Chaucyer on Ambassade into France,* in which he also called Thomas his "master dear," he made no allusion to Thomas's relationship to the poet. The one reference during his lifetime is in a 1396 suit brought by one Ralph Barton "versus Thomam Chaucer armigerum filium Galfridi Chaucer armigeri" ("against Thomas Chaucer esquire son of Geoffrey Chaucer esquire").[33] After Thomas's death in 1434, Thomas Gascoigne, the chancellor of Oxford University, writing about deathbed repentances, said that Geoffrey Chaucer in his last hours repented many of the things he had written, adding "Fuit idem Chawserus pater Thome Chawserus armigeri qui Thomas sepelitur in Nuhelm iuxta Oxoniam" ("The same Chaucer was the father of Thomas Chaucer esquire, which Thomas is buried in Ewelme near Oxford").[34] Thomas is, indeed, buried in Ewelme church, under a tomb bearing the Roet arms. One supposes that Ralph Barton and Thomas Gascoigne would have known what they were talking about. But neither one was as close to the royal household as Lydgate was, and Lydgate chose not to identify the relationship. Barton and Gascoigne sound as though they were voicing a common assumption.

However ideas of incest could have affected perceptions of Thomas's parentage, they have not always been successful in controlling human relations. Gaunt's solicitude for Philippa does seem unusual, and his influence would account for Thomas's brilliant marriage and amazing career. The possiblity that Geoffrey and Philippa's marriage was not ideal is reinforced by the fact that we do not know whether or for how long they lived together. Until 1374 it would appear that they lived in the royal and ducal households. In 1366 Philippa was awarded an annuity of ten marks by the king as a *domicella* of the chamber to Queen Phillipa, and in 1367 Geoffrey was awarded an annuity of twenty marks as an *armiger* (esquire) of the king's *familia.* In 1369 they were both granted royal allowances for clothing. In 1370 there are letters of protection for

Chaucer to go overseas in the king's service. Then in August 1372 there is a mandate for John of Gaunt's receiver to pay Philippa an annuity of ten pounds for her attendance upon Gaunt's second wife, Constance of Castile, which would seem to indicate that Philippa had shifted after the death of Queen Philippa in 1369 to service in Gaunt's household.

This is the first of a series of grants and gifts from Gaunt that go on until Philippa's death in 1387. In November 1372 Geoffrey was issued a commission to travel to Italy in the king's service. He was away until May 1373. On 13 July John of Gaunt went off to lead a campaign in France, and during the summer grants were made to Chaucer still as a member of the king's household. But when Gaunt returned to London in April 1374, Chaucer was made independent. On 23 April he was given a royal grant of a pitcher of wine daily; on 10 May he was given an apartment over Aldgate rent-free; on 8 June he was appointed controller of wool customs in the port of London; and on 13 June he and Phillipa were granted yet another annuity of ten pounds by John of Gaunt, he for the services rendered the duke and she for the services rendered the duke's mother and his wife. By this time, King Edward was in his dotage and the court was dominated by John of Gaunt and Alice Perrers, so any arrangements for the Chaucers cannot have been made by the king himself. It appears that when Geoffrey returned from Italy in the spring of 1373 something was amiss (Philippa was pregnant?) that had to be corrected, and was corrected by these arrangements just as soon as John of Gaunt returned to England in April 1374. If Thomas Chaucer was born in 1374, he would have been fifteen when he entered Gaunt's household in 1389, just about Chaucer's age when he entered the household of the Countess of Ulster.

Did Philippa move out of court with Geoffrey in 1374? That remains problematical. His description of his life in the apartment over Aldgate during the years he was keeping the account books at the Wool Quay sounds like a bachelor's existence. In *House of Fame,* the eagle that has been sent by Jupiter to carry "Geffrey" up to the palace of Fame to hear "tidings [news] of love," says:

And also, beau sir, other thynges,
That is that thou hast no tydynges
Of Loves folk yf they be glade,
Ne of noght elles that God made.
And noght oonly fro fer contree
That ther no tydynge cometh to thee,
But of thy verray neyghebores,
That duellen almost at thy dores,
Thou herist neyther that ne this;
For when thy labour doon all ys
And hast ymad thy rekenynges [accounts],
Instede of reste and newe thynges,
Thou goost hom to thy hous anoon
And, also dombe as any stoon,
Thou sittest at another book
Tyl fully daswyd [dazed] ys thy look,
And lyvest thus as an heremyte [hermit],
Although thyn abstynence ys lyte [little].

(*HF* 643–60)

In 1373, 1380, and 1381, John of Gaunt gave gifts to Philippa. In 1379 her annuity was granted by John of Gaunt's receiver in Lincolnshire. From 1380 till her death in 1387, her annuity was finally drawn at the hand of her husband in London. But in 1386 she was again in the ceremony at Lincoln Cathedral with John of Gaunt's and Katherine's children.

Geoffrey may have found solace elsewhere. In May 1380, he secured a legal release from a suit for "raptus" from Cecily Champaign.[35] Despite arguments to the contrary, legal opinion holds that the word means what it says—that Chaucer had been sued for rape and had to seek legal quittance. Since the quittance came after the fact, this episode must have come about 1378–1379 when Philippa was receiving her annuity in Lincolnshire.

This gossip might have a bearing on Chaucer's place in the emergence of English. As discussed at the beginning of this chapter, English had not yet achieved status as a cultivated language. If the propriety of its chief exponent in court existed under any cloud, it could only reinforce suspicions about the propriety of the language itself. And then there were those fabliaux, which, as we will see in the last chapter, disquieted the fastidious right down to the 1940s. This association of Chaucer's domestic situation with the lack of prestige of English is pure supposition, but the distrust of Chaucer's fabliaux and the lack of any extant copies of Chaucer's poems made during his lifetime are documented facts. No contemporary ever hinted denigration of his marriage, much less denigration of his marriage and denigration of poetry in English, but there is so much that we do not know.

It would be natural for Chaucer to have begun writing poetry in French rather than in English.[36] If he did, none has come down that can with assurance be identified as his. But there is an interesting manuscript at the University of Pennsylvania dating from about 1400 containing 310 French courtly poems by Machaut and the other leading continental court poets of Chaucer's generation. Fifteen of these lyrics are headed by the initials "Ch" which might indicate that they are by Chaucer. But these pieces show no trace of the uniquely Chaucerian voice. They celebrate the refining effects of love that informed the courtly ideal. To quote only two stanzas from the first:

> *Entre les biens que creature humainne*   1
> *Puist acquerir pour vivre liement,*
> *C'est d'ensuir la vie souverainne*
> *D'Amours, qui est le droit commencement*
> *De toute honneur; et amoureusement*   5
> *Eslire dame honnorable a maistresse;*
> *Et endurer, soit pour joie ou tristresse,*
> *Son bon plaisir et gracieux vouloir;*
> *Et par ainsi demenant ceste vie*
> *Se puet en grace amoureuse veoir*   10
> *Dont tous biens vient et plaisance cherie.*

(Among the good things that a human being
May acquire to live happily
Is to follow the sovereign life
Of Love, which is the true beginning
Of all honor; and in accordancce with Love
To choose an honorable lady as his mistress;
And endure, whether for joy or sadness,
Her good pleasure and gracious will;
By thus leading this life,
Through the grace of Love he will be able to perceive
Whence come all benefits and delightful pleasures.)

Car il est vray qu'en l'excellente demaine   *1*
D'Amours regne gracieux Pensement,
Franchise, Honnour, Esperance hautainne,
Foy, Loyauté, Leesse, Esbatement;
Secours conforte Dangier prestement   *5*
Quant Escondit le requerant trop blesce;
Refus y maint par raisonnable adresce,
Et Loing Detry, pour les bons percevoir
Ou Pitié vaint quant Bonne Amour l'otrie;
Et la est Joie en signe de Vouloir,   *10*
Vie aduree et de Joye enrichie.[37]

(For it is true that in the excellent domain
Of Love reign gracious Thought,
Generosity, Honor, high Hope,
Faith, Loyalty, Joy, Diversion;
Succor quickly comforts Disdain
When Denial so wounds the suppliant;
Refusal remains by reasonable decorum,
And Long Delay, that he may appreciate the benefits
When Good Love allows Pity to overcome;
There is Joy in the mark of Desire,
A stable life enriched with Joy.)

There could be no clearer statement than this of the feudal and ethical courtly ideal, addressed as much to the lord and to the poet himself as to the lady. Chaucer never wrote an English poem that expressed the ideal this directly. "Womanly Noblesse,"[38] the ballade attributed to him that most resembles the spirit of the "Ch" poems in the Pennsylvania manuscript, employs words not found elsewhere in Chaucer, which raises questions about its authenticity. Other than this, the courtly ideal is always treated critically in Chaucer's poems. For example, the most exquisite statement is that by Criseyde in *Troylus and Criseyde* (4.1667–80), but it comes just before she defects to Diomede, which raises questions in the reader's mind about its sincerity. Chaucer's poems are replete with the language and sentiments of courtly love, but they always slide away from full endorsement. So it seems unlikely that the "Ch" poems are by Chaucer. They represent, rather, the sort of poems he assimilated in the Countess Elizabeth's household.

The opening lines of *Book of the Duchess,* the first poem that can be unequivocally assigned to Chaucer, show how he transmutes the French into English, and how he modifies the sentiment in the process. The lines are adapted from Froissart's *Le paradis amoureus,* a conventional paean to the power of love. Love is driving the speaker of the poem to insomnia:

> *Je sui de moi en grant mervelle*   1
> *Coument tant vifs, car moult je velle,*
> *Et on ne poroit en vellant*
> *Trouver de moi plus travellant,*
> *Car bien sachiés que par vellier*   5
> *Me viennent souvent travellier*
> *Pensees et merancolies*
> *Qui me sont ens ou coer liies.*
> *Et pas ne les puis desliier,*
> *Car ne voel la belle oubliier*   10
> *Pour quelle amour en ce travel*
> *Je sui entrés et tant je vel.*[39]

(I am in great wonder
how I live, for I am so wakeful,
and nobody can be found
more troubled than I am by wakefulness,
for I well know that in wakefulness
many troubling thoughts and melancholies
come to me
which are in me where my heart lies,
and I cannot rid myself of them,
because I don't want to forget the fair one
for whose love I have assumed
this labor, and am so wakeful.)

This introduction leads into a conventional "complaint" against the hardheartedness of la belle dame sans merci. Chaucer in *Book of the Duchess* paraphrases Froissart's opening lines (the words of French origin in Chaucer's verses are in italics):

I have gret wonder, be this lyghte,   1
How that I lyve, for day ne nyghte
I may nat slepe wel nygh noght.
I have so many an ydel thoght
Purely for *defaute* of slepe   5
That, by my trouthe, I take no kepe
Of nothing, how hyt cometh or gooth,
Ne me nys nothyng leve ner looth.
Al is ylyche [alike] good to me,
Joy or sorowe, wherso hyt be,   10
For I have felynge in nothynge,
But as yt were a mased [dazed] thynge,
Alway in *poynt* to falle adoun;
For sorwful *ymagynacioun*
Ys alway hooly in my mynde.   15

(*BD* 1–15)

Chaucer begins paraphrasing the French closely, but at line 10 where Froissart's poem introduces the beloved, Chaucer continues to expatiate on the insomnia of the persona brought on by unspecified "sorowful imaginings." The pun on "wholly/holy" (line 15) is the touch of genius, because Chaucer goes on to transform the conventional French *complaint d'amour* into an elegy on the death of Blanche, Duchess of Lancaster, the wife of John of Gaunt, in which the troubadour cliché of "dying for love" becomes a moving tribute to the love of the Black Knight for his dead lady. The *Book of the Duchess* is a pastiche of passages from half a dozen French *dits d'amour*—of its 1334 lines, 848, two out of every three, are direct translations from Machaut, Froissart, *Roman de la Rose,* and others.[40] But even this early, derivative piece handles French sentimentalism with irony.

We shall in a later chapter look more closely at the Chaucerian voice. It is enough to say here that virtually everything Chaucer wrote throughout his career is a translation or adaptation from French. His earliest training may have been in Latin, but when he translated *Boece* he worked from the French version of Jean de Meun rather than from Boethius directly, and when he translated the *Melibee* he worked from the French version of Renaud de Louens instead of from the Latin of Albertano de Brescia. He cited Petrarch's Latin version as the source of the Clerk's Tale in the *Canterbury Tales,* but it turns out upon examination that he again worked from an anonymous French translation of Petrarch. The closest parallels to the Parson's Tale, *Treatise on the Astrolabe,* and *Equatorie of the Planets* are Latin, but the style and vocabulary probably bespeak French versions that have not yet been identified.[41]

In all of these cases, it appears that Chaucer had before him both the Latin and the French, because there are some phrases that more closely resemble the Latin, but it was the French that he followed most consistently. The same thing is true of his Italian. Since he was sent twice to Italy on diplomatic missions, he must have known Italian, and Boccaccio was the source of his two "best-made" stories, *Troylus and Criseyde* (from Boccaccio's *Il Filostrato*) and the Knight's Tale (from Boccaccio's *Il Teseide*). Yet Robert Pratt found a French prose translation, *Le roman de Troyle,* that evidently served as Chaucer's working model.[42] Indeed, the only substantial poem for which a French pony has not been found is the Knight's Tale, and the probability is, in view of the evidence of the other works, that the French model for that has simply not yet been identified.

Scholars get awfully defensive about Chaucer's use of Latin and Italian sources, and my remarks are not intended to denigrate his learning. But I am here discussing Chaucer's importance in creating English literary language and English literature, and it is obvious that it was French that Chaucer was creating literary English out of, not Latin or Italian. In many respects, his most famous work, the *Canterbury Tales,* is simply an anthology of French materials rendered into English. His achievement was the "Englishness" of the idiom in which they are expressed.

In his book on *Chaucer's Early Poetry,* Wolfgang Clemen observes that "From the beginning it was Chaucer's intention to give the idiom of English poetry the entrée into court, to ennoble it after the French pattern."[43] The nature of this process is suggested by the statistics on Chaucer's French vocabulary that show the derivative early poems averaging fewer French words than the later and more independent ones. For example, *Book of the Duchess* uses 28.7 percent French words, *Parliament of Fowls* 34.4 percent, and *House of Fame* 37.3 percent, as compared with *Troylus and Criseyde* with 43.5 percent, and the Canterbury tales, depending on their style, from a low of 26.7 percent for the Miller's Tale to a high of 51.3 percent for the Parson's Tale, with the average about 40 percent.[44] This reveals how rapidly the ethos was changing during Chaucer's lifetime. As long as French speakers in England were culturally distinct and superior, the languages were kept separate. The *Oxford English Dictionary* indicates that before 1250, very few French words were adapted into English (again think of the situation in Ireland where English has become the language of most of the common people while adopting very few Irish words). By 1250, two generations after the loss of Normandy, English words begin to come in, and the high point of their importation is 1350–1400, exactly Chaucer's lifetime.[45]

The statistics indicate that when Chaucer first began to try to write sophisticated poetry in English, he was sensitive to the distinction between French and English and attempted consciously or subconsciously to use as purely a native vocabulary as possible, as in the opening lines of *Book of the Duchess* quoted above. At this stage, many of the French words were adopted directly from his literary sources. But as he progressed, he lost this self-consciousness and used more and more French words, many taken from the admininistrative and cultural vocabulary with which he and his bilingual audience were so familiar. Since 1066 English had been a domestic language. It simply did not have a vocabulary for culture and learning. But that vocabulary was readily available in the French that the court and bureaucracy used every day. So what developed as court and commerce began to turn to English was a Franglais in which most of the substantive vocabulary was French while the syntax and form words (articles, pronouns, prepositions, auxiliary verbs, and the like) remained English. By the *Canterbury Tales,* 51.8 percent of Chaucer's vocabulary is French, almost exactly the percentage we have today, 50.1 percent. Compare the French in the first fifteen lines of the General Prologue with the first fifteen of *Book of the Duchess* quoted above. Again, words of Romance origin are in italics. (We say "Romance" because modern dictionaries trace them whenever possible directly to Latin, and to Italian and Spanish, even though most of them came in through French. "Romance," derived from "Rome," originally meant colloquial Latin spoken by the common people [Vulgar Latin] in contrast to "Latin," the official written language; hence the "Romance languages." Since popular narratives were written in "Romance," they came to be called "romances"; since they were usually erotic, "romance" came to imply eroticism. But back to Chaucer:)

> Whan that *Aprill* with his shoures soote
> The droghte of *March* hath *perced* to the roote
> And bathed every *veyne* in swich *licour*
> Of which *vertu engendred* is the *flour;*
> Whan *Zephirus* eek with his sweete breeth

> *Inspired* hath in evry holt and heeth
> The *tendre* croppes and the yonge sonne
> Hath in the Ram his halfe *cours* yronne,
> And smale foweles maken *melodye,*
> That slepen al the nyght with open eye—
> So priketh hem *nature* in hir *corages*—
> Thanne longen folk to goon on *pilgrimages.*
> And *palmeres* for to seken *straunge* strondes
> To ferne halwes kowthe in sondry londes;
> And *specially* from every shires ende . . .
>
> (*CT* 1–15)

The substantive vocabulary is almost wholly French ("March" and "palmeres" preserve the Anglo-Norman forms instead of the Parisian French; until Chaucer, French "Averil" was the most common spelling in England, and Chaucer himself sometimes used it, but after 1400, the Latin spelling became most common; "Zephirus" is directly from Latin).

But prestige and French vocabulary were not all that Chaucer contributed to English. His cultivation of metrical prosody and French stanzaic forms have informed our idea of what poetry is. Metrical prosody is not native to English. All of the Germanic languages inherit the stressed rhythms of the alliterative tradition.[46] In this tradition only the stresses are counted, and the number of unstressed syllables between the stresses can vary enormously. The Mother Goose rhymes maintain this tradition. A line like "Jack Sprat could eat no fat" has four stresses; the phrase "could eat no" must be resolved into the same time and stress as "Jack," "Sprat," and "fat." If it is not, if all of the syllables are given equal stress, the line ceases to be poetry. This is the rhythm of *Beowulf* ("Hwaet we Gar-Dena in gear dagum") and of *Piers Plowman* ("In a somer sesoun whanne softe was the sonne") in which the stresses are often marked by alliteration and the unstressed syllables between them vary in number. In contrast, Latin verse counts all the syllables and distributes them regularly ("Arma virumque cano, Troiae qui primus ab oris"), which leads to its designation as metrical (that is, "counted").

The "feet" in Latin verse were composed of arrangements of long and short syllables rather than stresses, but the Latin hymns and popular poetry by the twelfth century had substituted stress for length and produced rhythms as schmaltzy as jazz. For example, from a goliardic song:

> Gaude vallis insignata,
> Vallis rosis redimita,
> Vallis flos convallium,
> Inter valles vallis una.[47]

(Hail, noted valley,
Valley circled with roses,
Valley flower of valleys,
Among valleys the only one.)

French verse, derived from Latin, was from the beginning metrical, and by the thirteenth century we find metrical lyrics in English, like the wonderfully musical

> An hendy hap ichabe yhent.
> Ichot from hevene it is me sent.
> From alle wymmen mi love is lent,
> And lyht on Alysoun.[48]

(A wonderful fortune have I grasped.
I believe it is sent me from heaven.
From all [other] women my love is taken
And lights on Alysoun.)

The irregular syllabification had made alliterative poetry natural and conversational, appropriate for long narrative recitations like *Beowulf* and *Piers Plowman*. The earliest Middle English metrical verses were highly rhythmic and intended to be sung, and in even as consummate achievements as the *Pearl* poems, the rhythm tends to become singsong and cloying. For reasons too complex to fathom (perhaps as subliminal as those that led to the decay of inflectional endings and the great vowel shift), the ears of the English public from the thirteenth century onward began to prefer metrical to stressed rhythm, which by the time of John Skelton had come to sound uncouth and childish, appropriate only for "nursery rhymes." What was needed was a poet who could incorporate the new sound in verse intended to be read in a conversational tone of voice. This is what Chaucer was able to do. It explains his influence on all poets in English since his time. All critics agree that modern English poetry begins with him.

We could speak technically about the more even accentuation produced by not reinforcing the stresses with alliteration, about the more flowing rhythm produced by the regular number of syllables, about the variety produced by varying the order of the stressed and unstressed syllables, about movement from the four-foot octosyllabic line in the early poems to the five-foot iambic pentameter in *Troylus and Criseyde* and *Canterbury Tales,* about the four-beat effect created in the five-foot line by having two rhetorical stresses on each side of the caesura with the fifth stress promoted from a word not carrying rhetorical stress (in "Whan that Aprill / with his shoures soote," the fifth stress must be promoted from either "with" or "his").[49] But these are exactly the devices that produced the melody of French court poetry, and eventually the four-part line of the six-foot French alexandrine, which is based on the alternation of heavier and lighter syllables, even though French prosodists are reluctant to speak about accentual stress.

In French meter married to English stress, Chaucer managed to recapture the conversational cadence that had been lost to English verse when the synthetic grammar of Old English disappeared. In particular, he introduced the iambic pentameter line into English verse. Old English verse, although it counted only four stresses, managed to convey a conversational rhythm because of the large number of unstressed syllables between the stresses. Early French poems had been dance songs (hence names like "ballade" from Late Latin *ballare,* to dance; and "carol" from French *carole,* a round dance; the songs provided the rhythm by which the dancers kept time). The 4:4 rhythm of the dances called for four-foot, octosyllabic rhythms. This was the rhythm of the typical French *chanson*. All Middle English metrical verse before Chaucer was octosyllabic, as were Chaucer's early poems like *Book of the Duchess* and *House of Fame*. But the classical Latin poetry of Virgil and Ovid, intended for recitation, not for dancing, had used conversational five-foot (pentameter, decasyllabic) rhythm instead of the schmaltzy four-foot, and the French court poets began to adopt decasyllabic lines for their ballades and *dits d'amour*. Guillaume de Machaut, who, as we shall observe in the next chapter, popularized most of the stanzaic forms, has forty-five ballades set to music, seven with octosyllabic lines, but ten with decasyllabic, and twenty-eight with lines of varying length. The other French court poets and Chaucer's friend John Gower all used decasyllabic lines in their French ballades, evidently thinking of them as pieces to be recited rather than sung. But none of these employed pentameter rhymed couplets for narrative verse.

The pentameter couplets for narration were suggested, but not actually introduced, by the Italian poets. On his first trip to Italy in 1374, Chaucer must have become acquainted with the pentameter couplets at the end of the *ottava rima* (stanzas rhyming *a b a b a b c c*) of the narrative poems by Boccaccio and others. On his return he imitated Machaut and the French poets—and his English friend, John Gower—in using pentameter lines in rhyme royal stanzas (*a b a b b c c*) for narration in *Parliament of Fowls,* and he continued to use it so in *Troylus and Criseyde,* the Man of Law's Tale, the Clerk's Tale, and elsewhere. For the French poets, the ballade was a lyric form; Chaucer's innovation was to use the pentameter rhyme royal ballade stanza like the *ottava rima* for narrative. His final step was to introduce the pentameter couplet, which became his most influential form. It was immortalized in the General Prologue to the *Canterbury Tales,* the Knight's Tale, and others of the best tales, and led eventually, through Hoccleve, Lydgate, and other fifteenth and sixteenth-century poets, to the pentameter blank verse of Shakespeare and Milton as the favorite metrical form for English narrative poetry. There is a library of argument as to the exact character of Chaucer's pentameter line, and as to what Elizabethan pentameter owes to it and what to Latin poetry directly. But no one denies that Chaucer introduced iambic pentameter into English poetry, which is tribute enough.

Chaucer was by taste a narrative poet and made little contribution to the evolution of lyric forms. There are eighteen short poems attributed to him, some of doubtful authenticity, but most of his stanzas are in narrative poetry. This might have influenced Spenser to write the *Faerie Queene* in stanzaic form, but Chaucer himself grew away from this practice, and it has not proved a great attraction for later poets.

Chaucer's great contributions to the emergence of the English language are his demonstration of its capacity and the idiom and nuance of his individual expression. But before we turn to these, we must examine his contribution to broadening the subject matter that could be treated in English.

2.

Chaucer and the Inns of Court

We have explored Chaucer's experiences in ducal and royal courts in which he absorbed French courtly culture and began transmuting it into English. His courtly connection, added to his native genius, gave prestige to his English poetry, even though not yet enough to justify the production of the sort of sumptuous manuscripts produced for the French court poets. But as the court audience came to accept that poetry in English might be refined and sophisticated, other writers, like his friend John Gower, were encouraged to do the same, and cultivated literature in English began to emerge.

However, the literature of court culture is only part, and perhaps the least important part, of Chaucer's contribution. It is his introduction of satire and realism and his experiments with philosophical and scientific prose that demonstrated the capacity of the language. Chaucer's range is as great as that of any writer in English, Shakespeare not excepted. No other writer ranges more widely from serious to comic, from spiritual to bawdy, from lyric to narrative, from poetry to philosophy and science. By the time he finished, the prejudice that English was not capable of expressing any kind of sentiment or conveying any kind of information could no longer stand. We turn now to the experiences that supplied this breadth.

The fragments of the Countess of Ulster's household accounts run from 1356 to 1359. In 1359 this phase of Chaucer's education came to an end, when he transferred from domestic service for the countess to military service for her husband, Prince Lionel.[1] Evidently Chaucer was in the company led by the prince in Edward III's campaign in northern France that began in August 1359 and culminated in the Truce of Brétigny in May 1360, by which it was agreed that King Jean of France, who had been captive in London since Poitiers in 1356, would be ransomed for three million gold crowns, and Edward III would be confirmed in full sovereignty over England's vast holdings south of the Loire. In return, Edward relinquished his claim to the French throne and to Normandy and other territories in the north of France. Much has been speculated about the nature of Chaucer's service in that inglorious campaign, but there is no documentary evidence. An intriguing possibility is that when the English were besieging Reims in December, Chaucer may somehow have got to meet Machaut and Deschamps who were in the city at the time, but this is unlikely given his lowly situation and the posture of the opposing forces.

At a trial in 1386, Chaucer gave evidence that he had seen Sir Richard Scrope bearing a contested coat of arms at Rethel near Reims in this campaign. At the beginning of his deposition, Chaucer gave his age as "xl ans et plus, armeez par xxvii ans"[2] ("forty years and more, having borne arms for twenty-seven years"). This is the best evidence we have about his age. Forty years and more would place his birth before 1346. He would have been about fourteen when he entered Countess Elizabeth's household as a page about 1356; so he would have been born about 1342 and have been seventeen years old when he went to war with Prince Lionel. The twenty-seven years he had borne arms works out exactly, since 1359 plus twenty-seven gives us 1386, the date of the trial.

By testifying that he bore arms, Chaucer indicates that his service was military, as does the fact that he was ransomed by the king on 1 March 1360. Ransom had become the raison d'etre for chivalric warfare by the fourteenth century. As Froissart's *Chroniques* and other accounts make clear, booty may have been the reward for commoners, but ransoms were the chief means of support for second or third sons of the gentry who were landless under the system of primogeniture. Fighting in steel armor was not a great deal more dangerous to life and limb than a modern football game in full pads (the enclosed lists of the tournaments have often been compared to football stadiums); the point of the combat was to take prisoners and collect the ransoms.[3] Ransoms, determined by the standing and wealth of the prisoners, were an accepted part of military expense. We noted the enormous size of King Jean II's ransom in the previous chapter. In William Farley's account book that records Chaucer's ransom, amounts are listed for another yeoman (*valettus*) of the Countess of Ulster and two yeomen of the queen, so that Chaucer's was paid by the king does not mean that he was yet in the royal household. He had simply become a player in the chivalric game. Like his father before him, he was qualifying himself for government service by military experience before he turned to activities more congenial to a merchant's son. The sixteen pounds paid for his ransom was less than the fifty for Richard Stury, still esquire (a rank above *valletus*) but soon to be knighted, and Chaucer's associate in the king's service throughout his life. But it was still more than for most of the other yeomen in the list who went for ten pounds, or for John de Champain, chaplain, who went for eight. On 7 May 1360, the peace of Brétigny was agreed upon and most of the English troops returned home. In October, when the leaders returned to Calais for the ratification of the treaty, Chaucer was again in attendance upon Prince Lionel. The last record we have of this phase of his education is three crowns nine shillings paid to him in October for carrying letters for the prince from Calais to England.

One characteristic of his writings that has been frequently remarked upon is what has been called "Chaucer's silences."[4] We shall in later chapters explore the emergence of realistic detail and the sense of the individual in Chaucer's poetry. But we must recognize these as literary devices, not as autobiographical candor. Nowhere in his writing does Chaucer make a verifiable reference to a personal experience. He traveled extensively throughout Europe, in the Low Countries, France, and Spain, and over the Alps into Italy. He lived through plagues, the French

wars, the Great Schism, the trial of Wyclif at St. Paul's, the Peasants
Revolt. He was at the center of government during the decline of
Edward III and gynarchy of Alice Perrers, the misrule of Richard II,
and the jockeying for power of John of Gaunt, Thomas of Woodstock,
and Henry Bolingbroke. He was still alive when Henry finally overthrew
Richard and assumed the throne. But virtually never in his writings is
there a reference to any of these events or experiences. It is no good
saying that medieval authors were less specific than modern authors.
The writings of Chaucer's contemporaries like John Gower, Thomas
Hoccleve, Eustache Deschamps, and Jean Froissart show that writers
could, if they wanted to, be highly autobiographical and make specific
references to persons and events. One of Chaucer's important contributions to English literature was mimesis—the creation of reality through
language. But this was for him strictly a literary device. It was not his
manner to comment on his personal experiences. Like the character
Placebo in his Merchant's Tale, he was a "court-man" all his life (*CT*
4.1492ff.), supercautious to never say anything that could offend his
superiors.

And so we have no specific references to Chaucer's military adventures. But they must have broadened his experience beyond his paternal
home in the Vintry and the countess's household in a series of castles,
and have begun to introduce him to the world of men. This world
probably comprised a little fighting and ransoming, and, for a literate
youngster, a lot of personal service and errand running. But if it was
like any other military environment, it involved a great deal of waiting
and boredom whiled away with ribald humor and bawdy story telling.
I do not mean to imply that the Vintry and castle were protected
environments, but Chaucer had been a boy when he left home, and the
"courtesy" of the castle was, as Henry Adams so eloquently described it
in *Mont-Saint-Michel and Chartres,* a deliberate program by women and
the church to subdue the locker room machismo of the battlefield. We
shall in due course have more to say about the comic naturalism that
Chaucer introduced into English literature, but let us say now that both

the chivalric idealism and comic realism are Chaucer's transformations from French into English. The *Book of the Duchess, Parliament of Fowls, House of Fame, Legend of Good Women,* and some of the finest tales of Canterbury, like the Knight's and Franklin's Tales, are transmutations of French courtly literature—enriched, of course, with Latin and Italian materials and techniques. But the fabliaux, which represent the finest achievement of his mature art, are likewise transmutations of a French genre. Aside from Chaucer's five, we have only one fabliau in English, *Dame Sirith* (and half a dozen or so "humorous tales" infinitely less effective even than *Dame Sirith*). This is not to say that the English haven't always told bawdy stories in both pubs and castles, but the bawdy story was not adopted as an art form in English until Chaucer.

There are some 350 of these verse anecdotes preserved in French.[5] Joseph Bédier, who first discussed them, argued that fabliaux represented the literature of the emerging bourgeoisie in contrast to romances which represented the literature of the aristocracy.[6] Modern critics are no longer willing to accept this social ascription since it can be shown that some of the French fabliaux were written by the same authors and for the same audiences as the romances and *dits d'amour.* It is the situation, they argue, not the audience, that determines the appropriateness of a genre. The same audience expects different kinds of entertainment in a drawing room and in a nightclub.[7] The expectations of the largely female audience in the Countess of Ulster's drawing room would be quite different from that of Prince Lionel's male entourage in battle garb camped before the walls of Reims in wretched winter weather.

Situation aside, the French fabliaux were heavily class based. As Henri Bergson has pointed out, laughter is a form of social control, a perception of our superiority to others.[8] We laugh at incongruity as a way of compelling it to congruity. The incongruity may be perceptual, like a clown's nose or a foreigner's clothes, or it may be conceptual, like a pun or a dirty joke. It was the lower classes who were considered incongruous in the Middle Ages. Medieval humor was at their expense.

In Rome the lowest class of citizens was called "proletarian," derived from *proles,* offspring, those whose only service to the state was bearing children. But with the disappearance of cities in the Dark Ages, the lowest class came to be equated with peasants. Warriors were aristocratic by birth; priests were aristocratic by ordination; peasants were the commoners. The attitude of the higher classes toward the lowest led to the semantic pejoration of all terms for peasant. The Saxon warriors were "earls," their peasants "churls," but the earliest *OED* citation for "churl" as a term of contempt is not until about 1300, in *Havelock the Dane.* Similarly the early Germanic word *bur* meant merely the inhabitant of a burgh, a village, a meaning preserved in the term for a person who lives close by, a "nigh bur" or "neighbor." But since most *burs* were peasants, the word came to mean peasant or farmer, preserved in German *Bauer,* which is the meaning when it was first introduced into English. Not until the sixteenth century does the *OED* record "boor" as meaning an ill-bred or unrefined person. The precocity of the French in making social distinctions is revealed in the early date of their pejoration. In France, the village was called not a burgh but a *vill,* and the peasant who lived in it the *villein.* In the earliest *OED* citation (1303), the term already meant a base-minded rustic. Terms designating country folk still undergo the same sort of pejoration—for example, yokel, bumpkin, hayseed, clodhopper. In the Middle Ages, as today, the peasant was regarded as inferior, incongruous, in need of correction.

In the early Middle Ages there were only two classes, gentle and common, and the merchants as commoners were at first associated with the peasants. Chaucer himself represented the emergence of a literate, cultivated middle class. But in both the French and Chaucerian fabliaux, the early prejudice prevailed. The "boorish" or "churlish" pranks (in French *tromperie,* in German *Schwank*) of peasants and merchants are the source of the comedy, which indicates that the audience for the fabliaux was still largely aristocratic—humor by the gentles at the expense of the bumpkins. As the middle class became more influential, humor turned less on class and perceptual pranks and more on psychology and conceptual incongruity (although never absolutely—the comedy of P. G. Wodehouse shares much of the prejudice of the fabliaux). This concern with the psychology of behavior, in which the eccentricities of the gentles can be more comic than the uncouthness of the commons, is the stuff of the novel, foreshadowed in Boccaccio's *Decameron* where, unlike the French fabliaux, virtually none of the tales are about peasants; kings, knights, bishops, priests, and rich merchants are hoodwinked and ridiculed for their personal misbehavior. We see this contrast in Chaucer's Miller's and Reeve's Tales, whose comedy turns on the churlishness and pranks of carpenters and millers, and his Merchant's Tale, which turns on the psychological indecorum of an old knight and his squire. But more of this in due course. Chaucer's brief excursus into the world of soldiers and campgrounds must have opened to him the locker room world that the courtly cult of love had been established to counteract.

The introduction to male society that began on the battlefield continued over the next six years in the inns of chancery and inns of court, England's schools of law and business administration. The record of payment for the delivery of Prince Lionel's letters in October 1360 is the last Chaucer document we have until he reappears traveling in Spain in May 1366. For six years he disappears from sight. The documentary evidence of his education in the inns of court comes much too late. In the biography attached to the 1598 edition of Chaucer's works—the first literary biography of an English author—Thomas Speght says that "Master Buckley did see a record in the same house [that is, the Inner Temple, one of the four inns of court] where Geffrye Chaucer was fined two shillingess for beatinge a Franciscane fryer in fletestreate." None of the original documents have survived, but William Buckley was keeper of the records of the Inner Temple in Speght's time, and so in a position to see such a notation.[9] The earliest records that do survive, from Lincoln's Inn, beginning 1422, show that squires of aristocratic households were indeed enrolled in the inns of court and that the offense and penalty are not uncommon. Fraternity life could be rowdy even then.

We know very little about the organization of the inns of court in

Chaucer's time. The first description was written by Sir John Fortescue about 1460—a hundred years after Chaucer would have been there—in a Latin essay, *De Laudibus Legum Anglie* (In Praise of the Laws of England), written for the education of Prince Edward, son of Henry VI. In spite of its length, Stanley Chrimes' translation of this account is worth quoting in full both for its own interest and as the best account we have of the first schools in England where laymen could study for a profession without taking holy orders. If nothing else, its opening paragraph shows the prestige French still enjoyed sixty years after Chaucer's death:

> [Chapter 48] In the Universities of England the sciences are not taught unless in the Latin language. But the laws of that land are learned in three languages, namely, English, French, and Latin; in English, because among the English the law is deeply rooted; in French, because after the French had, by duke William the Conqueror of England, obtained the land, they would not permit advocates to plead their causes unless in the language they themselves knew, which all advocates do in France, even in the court and parliament there. Similarly, after their arrival in England, the French did not accept accounts of their revenues, unless in their own idiom, lest they should be deceived thereby. They took no pleasure in hunting, nor in other recreations, such as games of dice or ball, unless carried on in their own language. So the English contracted the same habit from frequenting such company, so that they to this day speak the French language in such games and accounting, and were used to pleading in that tongue, until the custom was much restricted by the force of a certain statute; even so it has been impossible hitherto to abolish this custom in its entirety, partly because of certain terms which pleaders express more accurately in French than in English, partly because the declarations upon original writs cannot be stated so closely to the form of these writs as they can in French, in which tongue the formulas of such declarations are learned. Again, what is pleaded, disputed, and decided in the royal courts is reported and put into book form, for future reference, always in the French language. Also,

very many statutes of the realm are written in French. Hence it happens that the language of the people in France now current does not accord with and is not the same as the French used among the experts in the law of England, but is commonly corrupted by a certain rudeness. That cannot happen with the French speech used in England, since that language is there more often written than spoken. In the third language above mentioned, in Latin, are written all original and judicial writs, and likewise all records and pleas in the king's courts, and also certain statutes. Thus, since the laws of England are learned in these three languages, they could not be conveniently learned or studied in the Universities, where the Latin language alone is used.

But those laws are taught and learned in a certain public academy, more convenient and suitable for their apprehension than any university. For this academy is situated near the king's courts, where these laws are pleaded and disputed from day to day, and judgements are rendered in accordance with them by the judges, who are grave men, mature, expert and trained in these laws. So those laws are read and taught in these courts as if in public schools, to which students of the law flock every day in term-time. The academy, also, is situated between the site of those courts and the City of London, which is the richest of all cities and towns of that realm in all the necessaries of life. And that academy is not situated in the city, where the tumult of the crowd could disturb the students' quiet, but is a little isolated in a suburb of the city, and nearer to the aforesaid courts, so that the students are able to attend them daily at pleasure without inconvenience of fatigue.

[Chapter 49] But, prince, in order that the form and arrangement of this academy may be clear to you, I will now describe it as far as I can. For there are in this academy ten lesser inns, and sometimes more, which are called Inns of Chancery [*hospicia cancellarie*]. To each of them at least a hundred students belong, and to some of them a much greater number, though they do not always gather in them all at the same time. These students are indeed, for the most part, young men learning the originals and something of the elements of law, who, becoming proficient therein as they mature, are absorbed into the greater inns of the academy, which are called the Inns of Court [*hospicia curie*]. Of these greater inns there are four in number [Lincoln's Inn, Gray's Inn, Middle Temple, and Inner Temple—the one Buckley identified as Chaucer's] and some two hundred students belong in the aforementioned form to the least of them. In these greater inns, no student could be maintained on less expense than £13 6s.8d. a year, and if he had servants to himself alone, as the majority have, then he will by so much the more bear expense. Because of this costliness, there are not many who learn the laws in the inns except the sons of nobles. For poor and common people cannot bear so much cost for the maintenance of their sons. And merchants rarely desire to reduce their stock by such annual burdens. Hence it comes about that there is scarcely a man learned in the laws to be found in the realm, who is not sprung from noble lineage. So they care more for their nobility and the preservation of their honour and reputation than others of like estate.

In these greater inns, indeed, and also in the lesser, there is besides a school of law, a kind of academy of all the manners that the nobles learn. There they learn to sing and to exercise themselves in every kind of harmonics. They are also taught there to practise dancing and all games proper for nobles, as those brought up in the king's household are accustomed to practise. In the vacations most of them apply themselves to the study of legal science, and at festivals to the reading, after divine services, of Holy Scripture and of chronicles. There is indeed a cultivation of virtues and banishment of all vice.

So for the sake of the acquisiton of virtue and discouragement of vice, knights, barons, and also other magnates, and the nobles of the realm place their sons in these inns, although they do not desire them to be trained in the science of the laws, nor to live by its practice, but only by their patrimonies. Scarcely any turbulence, quarrels, or disturbance ever occur there, but delinquents are punished with no other punishment than expulsion from communion with their society, which is a penalty they fear more than criminals elsewhere fear imprisonment and fetters. For a man once expelled from one of these societies is never received into the fellowship of any other of those societies. Hence the peace is unbroken and the conversation of all of them is as the friendship of united folk.[10]

The inns of chancery and of court provided the sort of training that would have been appropriate for both Chaucer's bureaucratic and literary careers, and also, as I shall argue, the most appropriate audience for his "non-courtly" prose and poetry.

Fortescue was describing the situation somewhat idealistically and from the vantage of 1460. We can only infer what the situation would have been in the 1360s when Chaucer might have attended. The medieval university was essentially a guild, in many ways like the merchants' and artisans' guilds, and the inns of chancery and of court were likewise guilds. As with other guilds, the principle of indoctrination was for the student to live in the house of the master and learn by apprenticeship (as in Chaucer's Cook's Tale; there are so few references to the evolution of the law inns in the fourteenth century that historians take Chaucer's description of the Manciple "of a Temple" in the General Prologue to *Canterbury Tales* as a documentary source!). Law, from Roman times on, implied writing. In Roman law, a formal order from the emperor or executive was termed a *brevis*, in English a "brief," so called, according to Bracton, because it "briefly" expressed the intention of the framer. Significantly, *brevis* came to be translated in English as "writ," which in Old English had meant simply a piece of writing. The twelve "masters of chancery" were the only authorities in England empowered to originate new language for royal and parliamentary writs.

Evidently in Chaucer's time, each of these major clerks had his own house in which lived apprentice clerks and candidates for clerkship.[11] These *hospiciae cancellarie* and *hospiciae curie* were at first merely the residences of the senior clerks (etymologically "inn" means "habitation" or "residence"). Lincoln's Inn was built on the ruins of Blackfriars' monastery, which had become part of the estate of Henry Lacy, Earl of Lincoln. Gray's Inn was in the former residence of the lords Gray of

Wilton. The other two inns of court, the Middle and Inner Temple, were in properties given to the Hospitalers of St. John when the Knights Templars had been suppressed in 1314, and rented by the Hospitalers to the law students sometime after 1324. The inns of chancery, except for Staple Inn, Chester Inn, and New Inn, all bore the names of their originators: Bernard's Inn, Thavie's, Clement's, Clifford's, Furnival's, and Lyon's.

The inns of chancery were the preparatory schools for the inns of court down to the eighteenth century.[12] There aspirants to the law and business administration learned the mysteries of writs and pleas and the formal procedures of administration. The distinction between the elite aspirants to the bar and those who had no hopes of ever moving on to the inns of court are made clear in the *Ordinaciones cancellarie domini regis facte anno duodecimo regni regis Ricardi secundi* (The ordinations of the royal chancery established in the twentieth year of the reign of King Richard II [1397]) through which we know something of the organization of chancery in Chaucer's time. These rules forbad the aspirants to the law from mingling with the "ordinary clerks"—"omnes allei clerici qui dicte cancellarie propter doctrinam et scripturam adhererere voluerint" ("all the other clerks who want to adhere to the said households of chancery for doctrine and writing").[13] "Writing" no doubt meant the technical forms of writs about which we will say more in a moment, but it also meant the formal chancery hand in which all records had to be inscribed. Without this mechanical skill, equivalent to typing, or today to computer literacy, Chaucer could not later have been appointed as controller of customs in London with the provision that "rotulos suos dicta officia tangentes manu sua propria scribat" ("that he write the rolls touching said office in his own hand"),[14] and we know he had mastered it because this is the hand of what we take to be his holograph *Equatorie of the Planets*.

The normal period of residence in an inn of chancery was three years, which would account for 1360–1363 in Chaucer's education. From there most clerks went directly to work as apprentices in various offices and households. Acceptance into one of the inns of court was acceptance into a way of life, like membership in a gentleman's club or a fellowship in an Oxford college. The inns had been originally established as guilds or societies for practicing lawyers who maintained residences and offices there as long as they lived—as indeed they still do. As Fortescue indicated, residence in an inn did not necessarily imply study or practice of law. Entering members did not even begin to study law until their second or third year of residence, and Philip Smith in his *History of Education for the English Bar* expresses some mystification as to what students did for their first two or three years.[15] He supposes that they continued their general education in classical literature, law French, diplomatics, handwriting, and the like. It was evidently these three years that Chaucer spent at the Inner Temple (1363–1366), leaving just at the time he would have begun his professional study of law.

Quite as important as what he learned at the inns of court would have been the friends he made there. These would remain his circle of associates throughout his life.[16] London in the fourteenth century was a city in which everybody of importance knew everybody else of importance—as they still seem to do today. Estimates of population are very sketchy, but the total seems to have been only some forty thousand in Chaucer's time. The higher nobility consisted of about a dozen families whose members and dependents lived mostly outside of London in castles on their feudal estates. Most of the 60 percent of the land not in the hands of the monasteries was owned by some 50 *magnates regni*. All of these had London residences, like the Savoy Palace of John of Gaunt or Westminster Palace of the king, attended by scores if not hundreds of clerks, yeomen, and *garcouns* (common servants). Beneath these was a large knightly class of landowners seen seldom in London but often on the battlefield. Chancery in Westminster Hall and in the Rolls House on Chancery Lane served as the secretariat for all branches of government and the law (the two were not clearly distinguished). It was officially composed of only 120 clerks, served, of course, by scores if not hundreds of apprentice clerks and servants. Sylvia Thrupp, in *The*

Merchant Class of Medieval London, estimates that in 1501 there were about two thousand merchants in livery in the city[17] (vintners, grocers, fishmongers, and the like), twenty-four hundred artisans in livery (glovers, carpenters, clothworkers, scriveners, and the like), with perhaps another two thousand citizens of lower rank. If each of these sixty-four hundred had a wife, a child, an apprentice, and a servant—and most would have more than this—the total swells to some thirty thousand. There were 120 religious institutions (churches, monasteries, hospitals, and so on) in the city, again with a minority in full orders and many apprentices (in the monasteries they would be called novitiates) and servants.

The bishops, abbots, priests, and clerks attached to the religious establishments in London and throughout England were the remnant of the "Caesarian clergy" that had administered government throughout Europe since the fall of Rome, whose displacement by educated laymen is the story of the Renaissance. Chaucer, like Dante and Petrarch, is a product of this evolution. Much of the conflict during the reign of Richard II was the result of struggle for the control of government between the inns of court lay party and the bishops who still served as royal chancellors and secretaries. As we shall see, this struggle may be reflected in the ordering of the pilgrims in the General Prologue to the *Canterbury Tales,* in which the Knight heads the catalog of the estates instead of an ecclesiastical primate of the sort that usually heads such lists.[18] Chaucer was one of this party of "new men" who were beginning to take over the government.

No records exist of the members of the inns of court before the Black Book of Lincoln's Inn that begins in 1422, but it is Speght's tradition that there is where Chaucer met such friends as the poet John Gower and the lawyer Ralph Strode. Gower is second in importance only to Chaucer in development of literary English. Although his collection of stories, *Confessio Amantis,* is not the most scintillating of productions, it exemplifies the same scope and fluency as Chaucer's and helped to establish the prestige of English as a literary language. Gower had earlier written two long poems in Latin and French, and the Latin title *Confessio Amantis* for his English work suggests his lingering doubt about the legitimacy of English. The similarity of the prologue of the *Confessio* to the prologue of Chaucer's *Legend of Good Women* suggests that it was Chaucer's example that encouraged him finally to write in English.[19] The encouragement appears to have been indirect. Gower attributes his writing in English to the express command of King Richard, as described in the previous chapter. If this account is true—and why should it not be?—it suggests that Chaucer's example may have begun to persuade Richard and Anne that English was a legitimate language for cultivated poetry, and that as a result they commissioned the two premier poets of the nation to compose in English collections of stories about love derived largely from the classics. Gower was evidently independently wealthy. He never held public office, but he tells us that he was a lawyer and his life records are a long series of property transactions. When Chaucer went abroad in 1378 he gave his power of attorney to Gower, which speaks well both for their friendship and for Gower's legal competence. And the only specific dedication in any of Chaucer's writing is to Gower and Strode:

> O moral Gower, this bok I directe
> To thee, and to thee, philosophical Strode,
> To vouchen sauf ther [where] nede is to correcte
> Of youre benygnites and zeles goode.
>
> (*TC* 5.1856–59)

Ralph Strode is a tantalizing figure. Recent scholarship accepts the identity of the fellow of Merton College (1359–1360) and the London lawyer (1373–1387).[20] The transition from Oxford logician to London lawyer is as unlikely as Chaucer's own education in the inns of court, but the offices Strode held for the Corporation of the City of London— Common Serjeant (public prosecutor 1373–1382) and Standing Counsel (1386–1387)—would have been unlikely without training in an inn of chancery and membership in an inn of court. Strode's life records have the same gap as Chaucer's. Strode's Oxford records end in 1360, the same year that Chaucer's end in Prince Lionel's household. Presumably they both entered the inns of chancery in that year and proceeded to the inns of court after two or three years. Chaucer dropped out in 1366, but Strode continued his legal education until he was called to the bar and ready to pursue his legal career after 1370. In the mid-1380s Chaucer dedicated *Troylus and Criseyde* to him and to John Gower. Strode and Chaucer must have been friends until Strode died in 1387, and it could have been he who introduced Chaucer to the study of astronomy.

Thomas Usk, author of *Testament of Love* that borrowed from Chaucer's *Boece, House of Fame,* and *Troylus,* was likewise an attorney and involved in city politics. Although his quotations are important evidence that Chaucer's works circulated in writing during his lifetime, it is questionable whether his acknowledgments would have done much to raise the prestige of English poetry. What we know about his professional life is not attractive.[21] He began as a lollard but recanted when he found that belief was likely to be dangerous. He served as confidential clerk to John of Northampton, mayor of London, and was arrested and imprisoned in order to induce him to reveal secrets that would implicate Northampton. This he did, testifying before the king at Reading in 1384. He then joined the party of Nicholas Brembre, the next mayor of London and supporter of Richard, only to be accused by Thomas of Gloucester and the appellant lords and executed for treason along with Brembre in 1388. The conflict between King Richard and Thomas of Gloucester, 1385–1389, for control of the government was murky. In the process, many of the king's supporters were killed or punished. Chaucer himself lost his controllership of customs and his royal annuities. The approbation of Chaucer's English writings by one of the unfortunates executed in the process cannot have greatly bolstered either Chaucer or his English poetry in court circles.

We do not know how many of the other officials that Chaucer served with over the years may have had training in the inns of court— William Beauchamp, King's Chamberlain; Richard FitzAlan, Earl of

Arundel; Simon Burley, tutor to young King Richard; Richard Stury, ransomed in 1360 along with Chaucer and with him on missions to France and on commissions to repair the walls and ditches in Kent. The list could go on and on. As Fortescue pointed out and as Sylvia Thrupp has documented,[22] the royal court, inns of court, and wealthy merchants of London were beginning to intermarry and enter into corporate business ventures (purchase of property, export of wool and grain, and the like) in Chaucer's time. These groups formed an educated, secular, bourgeois audience for sophisticated poetry in English.

Fortescue's description makes it evident how unusual it would have been for a merchant's son to be enrolled in the inns of court, but this would have been no more unusual than for the same merchant's son to have served as a page in a princely household. Chaucer's education tells us a great deal about the resources and influence of his vintner father, John Chaucer. As Fortescue's description also makes clear, the inns of court and of chancery were more nearly fraternities than they were schools. The educational part was tutorial, carried on by "writing masters," and then by apprenticeships ("clerkships") in appropriate offices. The writing masters were independent entrepreneurs (like music teachers today) who instructed students not only at the inns but also at Oxford and Cambridge.[23] They taught the chancery hand in which all official documents had to be inscribed, the art of composing in Latin and French (significantly not in English), and the art of composing letters and documents in appropriate forms and styles. Their tool was the formulary, which, as we shall see, may have suggested to Chaucer the novel feature of the *Canterbury Tales*.

There were no final examinations or degrees at the inns. Any testing would come only after years of apprenticeship. We have beginning with 1580 the admission rolls for the "cursitors" in chancery, that is, the clerks of the second class who kept the rolls and issued writs under the direction of the masters in chancery. The cursitors eventually developed into the solicitors in the English legal hierarchy who do the paper work for the law, as contrasted with the barristers who appear in court. The admission

rolls record samples of the chancery hand of the applicants and their
knowledge of the forms of writs, followed by a set formula:

> To Lord Chancellor. Our duties in most humble wise considered,
> may it please your honour to be advertized that according to the
> accustomed manner heretofore in that behalf used, we whose names
> are hereunder written have examined Richard Crosse, one of the
> Clerks of John Symond Esq, one of the Cursiters of the high court of
> Chauncery, who hath served under the said John Symond as his clerke
> in his office of a cursitere by the space of eleven yeares, who as well
> for his honest character as for his skill in the course of common
> practise and also for his faire writing, now find to be sufficient and fit
> person to be admitted to execute the office of cursiter.[24]

Those students who became advocates clerked and read law in an advo-
cate's office, likewise for many years, until they were deemed sufficiently
prepared and mature to be called to the bar and so become barristers,
as advocates were designated.[25] If they became "serjeants of the law" or
judges, they might become "benchers" in their inns.

But these educational activities were conducted for a minority of
the residents and aside from the fraternity life. The principal function
of the inns was to provide communal housing and dining for the members, and revels whenever an excuse could be found. Again, we have no
records of the merrymaking until the sixteenth century, only Fortescue's
remarks about singing and dancing and festivals. As A. W. Green records
in *The Inns of Court and Early English Drama*, by 1505 the Inner Temple
had a "master of the revels" (*magister jocorum*) whose responsibility it
was to organize the feasts and entertainment.[26] From the sixteenth
century on, there are extensive records of various kinds of revels: professional revels (feasts in connection with law lectures and moot courts and
the promotion of members to sergeancies); political revels (in connection with royal tournaments, marriages, anniversaries); and ecclesiastical
revels on holidays ("holy days," the etymological source of the word,
particularly Christmas, when there were great feasts at which the gentle-

men of the inns were entertained with music and dance, and eventually with masques and dramas). Some of the first Elizabethan plays like *Gorboduc, Jocasta,* and *The Supposes* were written by and presented for the members of the inns of court. Shakespeare's *Comedy of Errors* was first presented at Gray's Inn in 1594 and *Twelfth Night* at the Middle Temple in 1602. Writers have continued to live in the inns and draw upon them for material, like Thackery in *Pendennis* and Dickens in so many of his novels.

The revels were no doubt more formal by the time of Henry VIII than in the time of Edward III, but we may be sure that like the monasteries and craft guilds, the lawyers' guilds from their inception enjoyed their versions of Bakhtinian festive comedy. We cannot be positive that Chaucer attended the inns of court, but the circumstantial evidence is persuasive, and the revels of the inns would have provided the best audience for most of his poetry and prose.

It is surprising how few of Chaucer's poems bear clear marks of being addressed to royalty. The first is the early (1368) *Book of the Duchess,* an elegy on the death of Blanche of Lancaster, wife of John of Gaunt, third son of Edward III, and mother of Henry Bolingbroke, the eventual Henry IV. She and Gaunt appear to be identified when the poem ends beside "A longe castel with walles white, / Be Seynt Johan, on a ryche hille" (l.1318–19; "long castel"=Lancaster, "white"=Blanche, "Seynt Johan"=John, "ryche hille"=Richmond; John of Gaunt was Earl of Richmond before he married Blanche and became Duke of Lancaster). The second royal dedication is even more oblique, when at the end of the prologue to the *Legend of Good Women* Alceste, the queen of love, commands the author "whan this book ys maad, yive it the quene, / On my byhalf, at Eltham or at Sheene" (F496). Eltham and Shene were royal palaces in Kent which King Richard and Queen Anne particularly favored. Richard was so affected by Anne's death in 1394 that he had Shene manor torn down, and these two lines were excised when the prologue was revised, perhaps for Richard's second marriage in 1396 to the seven-year-old Princess Isabel of France. Other than these, there

are two ballades to royalty.[27] One addressed to "conquerour of Brutes
Albyoun" is accepted as being a plea to Henry IV at his coronation to
renew Chaucer's pension. Another exhorting "O prince" to rule more
equitably was identified by John Shirley long after Chaucer's death as
addressed to King Richard. Speght in his edition also asserted that the
very early translation from French, *Prier a Nostre Dame,* was composed
"at the request of Blanche Duchesse of Lancaster, as a praier for her
privat use," and modern critics have speculated that the lovely ballade
To Rosemounde may have been addressed to Princess Isabel. But already
we are getting into the realm of pure speculation. The fact is that the
one long poem, *Troylus and Criseyde,* and the three ballades whose
dedicatees are actually named are addressed to friends of the inns of
court crowd, John Gower, Ralph Strode, Sir Philip de la Vache, "Mais-
ter" Bukton, and Henry Scogan.[28] Although Chaucer was in his own
time and is still today regarded as a court poet, the evidence is that most
of his verse and prose was addressed to the new bourgeoisie.

   We do not know the occasions or audiences for any of the non-
courtly pieces, but their quizzical tone and growing sophistication are
those of an observer sharing with equals his bemusement at the personalities and processes of government rather than of a subordinate addressing patrons. The poet-persona in *Book of the Duchess* and *Legend of
Good Women* does adopt this abject role. The two poems that follow
Book of the Duchess, House of Fame and *Parliament of Fowls,* are generally
accepted as dealing with the six years of negotiating it took to find a
wife for King Richard who was eleven years old when he ascended the
throne in 1377.[29] Chaucer was directly involved in these negotiations. In
1377 Froissart records "Jeffrois Chauciés" along with Sir Richard Stury
and others at Montreuil-sur-Mer in France in abortive negotiations for
Richard to marry Princess Marie of France. In 1378 Chaucer traveled
to Italy, presumably in connection with the abortive negotiations for
Richard to marry Caterina, daughter of Barnabo Visconti, ruler of
Milan. Finally in 1381 Richard was betrothed to Anne, sister of Wences-
las, king of Bohemia and emperor of the etheric Holy Roman Empire.

In a later chapter we will examine the themes and treatments in some detail, but the point I want to make now is that the attitude of the two poems is that of a critical observer, not of an obsequious participant.

In *House of Fame* the dreamer describes his employment in the custom house where Chaucer served from 1374 to 1385, and pokes fun at his bookishness and unsociablity, and perhaps at his domestic discord, in a fashion that would be most amusing to those who knew him personally. The eagle says that he has been sent to take him to the house of Fame to learn "tydynges / Of Loves folk" (*HF* 644–45). "Tidings" meant "news"; "news about Love's servants" would be an appropriate description of the commission of envoys in search of a bride for the prince. Twelve times more in the poem, the eagle says that he is carrying the dreamer to where he will hear "loves tydynges." When he learns nothing in the house of Fame the friendly eagle deposits him in the house of Rumor. He hears a commotion "in a corner of the halle, / Ther men of love-tydynges tolde" (*HF* 2142–43) and sees

> a man,
> Which that y nevene nat kan [I cannot name],
> But he semed for to be
> A man of gret auctorite. . .
>
> (*HF* 2155–58)

And here the poem breaks off. Most students take this inconclusive ending as testimony to the frustration of the seemingly never-ending search for "tydynges" about Richard's marriage.

Chaucer's first poem in pentameters, *Parliament of Fowls,* may be earlier or later than *House of Fame,* but it shows the same frustration. Here the dreamer is led by Scipio Africanus rather than by the eagle, and on a quest for "comoun profyt" instead of tidings of love. "Common profit" was becoming an important concept in political philosophy as medieval plutocracies groped towards a more participatory commonwealth. The Peasants Revolt, which was just brewing or just past when the *Parliament* was being composed, turned on exactly this concept.

Chaucer, from his apartment over Aldgate leading to Mile End, could have watched the drama as Richard brought the Revolt to an end on 14 June 1381 by boldly addressing the peasants in English. Chaucer never commented directly on such actual events, but Richard's behavior at Mile End was widely acclaimed, and a marriage for the boy-king would certainly contribute to the common profit of an English population deeply divided. As a matter of fact, Anne did prove to be a steadying influence, and it was only after her death in 1394 that Richard began really to self-destruct.

In the *Parliament,* Scipio first leads the dreamer into the Temple of Love where he perceives the futility of obsession with sterile courtly love—the culture Chaucer had absorbed in the Countess of Ulster's household. From there he goes out into a glade where Dame Nature is assigning the birds their mates on St. Valentine's Day. What follows is a delightful burlesque on the endless palaver of diplomatic negotiations. The arguments between the royal fowls and the common fowls would be most amusing to the inns of court crowd who were constantly involved in just such debates in the law courts, in Parliament, and in diplomacy. The proclivities revealed by speech and behavior of the birds are exactly what a lawyer is most trained to observe. Chaucer had shown lawyerly sensitivity to the nuances of language by commenting on the Black Knight's modest manner in *Book of the Duchess* (529–31) and the eagle's various manners in *House of Fame* (561–66, 865–69). Here he is careful to poke just as much fun at the speech and behavior of the common birds as at that of the royals. And the upshot, when the "formel" (female) eagle asks respite because she is not ready to serve either "Venus or Cupide," is just as inconclusive as the *House of Fame.*

The stage of the negotiation this refusal embodies is not clear, but I find most probable Haldeen Braddy's hypothesis that it refers to the 1376–1378 negotiations for Princess Marie. This bargaining was fraught with black comedy. Poor Marie, age five, died in 1377 just as the treaty with the French was about to be ratified, and negotiations were transferred to her three-year-old sister Isabel, who also died, at which point negotiations were transferred to the French king's infant daughter just born in 1378. If *Parliament of Fowls* does refer to this sequence, there is more than a trace of bitterness in the plea of the formel eagle for respite.[30]

The chronology of Chaucer's poems is by no means certain, but *Troylus and Criseyde* and *Palamon and Arcite* (later included in the *Canterbury Tales* as the Knight's Tale) are generally accepted as coming next after *House of Fame* and *Parliament of Fowls*. The Knight's Tale is Chaucer's most straightforward presentation of the chivalric ideal, but it is structured around the definition of law at the beginning of the *Corpus juris civilis,* the codification of Roman law upon which canon law was based. The *Corpus* begins by distinguishing three kinds of law: natural law (*lex naturalis*), the law of peoples (*lex gentium*), and civil law (*lex civilis*). The desire of Palamon and Arcite for Emelye exemplifies natural law—sex, propagation of the species, which we share with animals. The tournament Theseus arranges to determine which one will marry her exemplifies the law of peoples—might makes right, to the victor go the spoils. The parliamentary settlement by which Palamon finally marries Emelye exemplifies civil law—negotiation and equity. So this courtly romance has been adapted to reflect Chaucer's experiences in law school.

The subject of *Troylus and Criseyde* is likewise courtly love. But its source was a novella by Boccaccio rather than a French courtly romance. We have already observed that in the *Decameron* Boccaccio had moved from the conventional, class-based humor of the fabliaux towards individualism and psychology. His *Il Filostrato* similarly moves from the conventional motivation of the courtly romance in the direction of the psychological motivation of the novel. Chaucer's assimilation of this psychology in the portrayals of Criseyde and Pandarus is what has led critics to call *Troylus and Criseyde* the first English novel. But C. S. Lewis and others have argued that the portrayal of Troylus himself moves Chaucer's poem back towards the conventionality of the romance.[31] In *Filostrato* Troylus is a normal, aggressive youth, as Criseyde is a normal, receptive girl. In Chaucer's version he is as hesitant as Lancelot before Guinevere. His feckless lack of initiative makes him as nearly a laughing-stock as the eagles are laughingstock to the common fowl in *Parliament of Fowls*. So if *Troylus* was intended for a court audience, it was different from the audience for the "Ch" poems and *Book of the Duchess* where the subservience of the chivalric lover is still pristine.

The *Legend of Good Women* came after *Troylus* as we can tell by the references to *Troylus* in its prologue. In many ways it returns to the romantic idealization of love of the "Ch" poems and *Book of the Duchess,* perhaps because its subject matter and tone were dictated by Richard and Anne. Its prologue parallels closely the prologue to John Gower's *Confessio Amantis.* In that prologue we have the delightful account of Gower's taking a water taxi across the Thames and meeting the royal barge. He is called onto the barge and commanded by the king to write a "boke / That he himself it mihte loke." This was the inspiration for a collection of stories entitled "The Lover's Confession" (*Confessio Amantis*). Gower's prologue then goes on to present the court of love presided over by the king and queen of love, popularized by Guillaume de Lorris in *Roman de la Rose,* and used for two centuries throughout Europe as an icon of the exclusivity and refinement of aristocratic society. The prologue to the *Legend of Good Women* is Chaucer's only presenta-tion of this icon. The appearance of the king and queen of love and their attitudes toward the poets in the two prologues are very similar. In the *Legend* it is the queen, Alceste, who commands the poet to write a series of legends about love's martyrs, and when the book is finished, "give it to the queen." The similarities suggest that Chaucer might have been on the royal barge at the same time as Gower, and that the two collections of classical love stories, both framed in the religion of love, might have been ordered by the royal couple at the same time.[32]

Another reason that the prologue to the *Legend* retreats to the courtly mode is that it is also a response to a complimentary ballade that Deschamps had sent to Chaucer, evidently in the spring of 1386, of which we may quote the first stanza:

O Socrates plains de philosophie,	O Socrates full of wisdom,
Seneque en meurs, et Auglux en pratique,	Seneca in morals, and Aulus Gellius in practical affairs,
Ovides, grans en ta poëterie,	Ovid, great in thy poetry,
Briés en parler, saiges en rethorique,	concise in speech, experienced in rhetoric,
Aigles treshaulz, qui par ta theorique	lofty eagle, who by thy science
Enlumines le regne d'Eneas,	dost illumine the kingdom of Aeneas,
L'isle aux geans (ceuls de Bruth) et qu'i as	the isle of giants (those of Brutus) and who there hast
Semé les fleurs et planté le rosier;	sown the flowers and planted the Rose-tree [translated the *Roman de la Rose*];
Aux ignorans de la langue pandras—	those ignorant of the language [French] thou wilt enlighten—
Grant translateur, noble Geffroy Chaucier	great translator, noble Geoffrey Chaucer.[33]

The next two stanzas and the refrain go on to praise Chaucer's translation of the *Roman de la Rose* and say that he is sending the poem to Chaucer by Sir Lewis Clifford.[34] This poem is biographically very important because it is one of the only two documents that link Chaucer the man of affairs with Chaucer the poet. Aulus Gellius, a second-century Roman judge, was famous in the Middle Ages both as an official and as the author of *Attic Nights,* a collection of quotations and commentary on law and antiquities. This and Chaucer's own self-portrait in *House of Fame* are the only references to his dual career.

The poem from Deschamps is the first international recognition ever accorded to an English poet. Eustache Deschamps, almost exactly Chaucer's age, held positions in the French court very similar to Chaucer's in the English court, so that his ballade had something of the force of a diplomatic missive. Although both were royal retainers and poets, it is noteworthy that Deschamps's poems circulated widely in both France and England during his lifetime in presentation manuscripts and other fine copies, while, so far as we can tell, not a single manuscript of Chaucer's poems was copied during his lifetime. This is further evidence of the prestige of French in comparison with English. The remarkable thing is that Deschamps was aware in 1386 of Chaucer's "translations," and recognized that he was enriching English poetry with material from Latin and French. Clearly his work was making its mark, even though no copies were yet circulating. Chaucer replied to Deschamps's compliments by acknowledging his indebtedness to the French court poets:

> For wel I wot [know] that ye han [have] her-biforne
> Of makyng ropen [reaped], and lad awey the corne,
> And I come after, glenyng here and there,
> And am ful glad yf I may fynde an ere
> Of any goodly word that ye han left.
> And thogh it happen me rehercen eft [say again]
> That ye han in your fresshe songes sayde,
> Forbereth [bear with] me, and beth nat evele apayde
> [displeased]
>
> (*LGW* 73–80)

The prologue to *Legend of Good Women* is, therefore, for several reasons, a return to the transmutation of French court poetry into English. But like the Knight's Tale, it is not entirely of the court. The concerns of the city obtrude in the sharpest criticism Chaucer ever made of the bad rule of Richard II, when Alceste scolds the God of Love for being like the "tyrants of Lombardy" who squander their wealth and mistreat their subjects (lines 352–408). In 1386 Richard's favorite, Michael de la Pole, Earl of Suffolk (whose grandson married the daughter of Thomas Chaucer), was removed by Parliament from the chancellorship for misappropriation of public funds, and a commission of eleven regents was appointed to reform abuses in government. So the poem speaks with unusual frankness about a political crisis.[35]

But this was not Chaucer's way. His final poetic effort was devoted to his most influential work, the *Canterbury Tales,* and the structure of this collection reflects the greatest influence of his inns of court experience. The most remarkable stylistic innovation of the *Canterbury Tales,* and the one that has most influenced later English writing, is the creation of different voices, personalities, and points of view for the different pilgrims. There are many collections of stories from the Middle Ages, the *Golden Legend* and Boccaccio's *Decameron* among the most famous. But none of them uses the dramatic technique of matching the subjects and styles of the stories to the personalities of their tellers—a knight telling a courtly romance, a miller telling a bawdy fabliau, a prioress telling a miracle of the Virgin. Ever since the encomiums of Dryden and Blake, this has been recognized as Chaucer's greatest achievement. Where did it come from?

It came from the *ars dictaminis.* The original craft of *ars dictaminis* was letter writing, and the aim of letter writing, as set forth in the earliest treatise on the subject, by Alberic of Monte Cassino in Italy in 1087, was to secure the good will of the recipient by making the style and language appropriate to his condition.[36] We recall that before he begins to describe the Pilgrims in the General Prologue, Chaucer promises to tell us "al the condicioun / Of ech of hem; so as it semed me, / And whiche [what] they weren, and of what degree" (37–40). The textbooks for teaching *ars dictaminis* were "formularies," collections of model letters appropriate for any occasion. The earliest collection, compiled in 1119, offers sixteen models addressed to different kinds of recipients:

A papa ad imperatorem (from pope to emperor)
Ab imperatore ad papam (from emperor to pope)
Ab episcopo ad papam (from bishop to pope)
A papa ad episcopum (from pope to bishop)
Ab episcopo ad subditos (from pope to subordinates)
A subditos ad episcopum (from subordinates to bishop)
Ad episcopum ab episcopo (from bishop to bishop)
Item ad episcopum (another to a bishop)

Ad discipulos scienciam magistrum petentes (to scholars
   seeking wisdom from a teacher)
Ad magistrum (to a teacher)
Ad patrem (to a father)
Ad amicum (to a friend)
Ad abbatem vel monachum (to an abbot or a monk)
Ad fratrem (to a brother)
Ad militem (to a soldier)
Civitas ad civitem, inimici aut amici (city to city, hostile
   or friendly)

We have many such formulary collections from all over Europe, mostly
in Latin, but occasionally in French and other vernaculars. We have
none in English, although late in the fifteenth century a few English
letters began to creep in. Thomas Hoccleve, Chaucer's disciple, after
working for thirty-five years in the privy seal office of chancery, spent
his years of retirement (1423–1425) compiling a formulary of privy seal
missives that is still extant.[37] Although he wrote poetry in English, all of
the examples in his formulary are in Latin and French. Hoccleve was
making his compilation after the death of Henry V, when chancery was
already in the process of shifting over to English, but he obviously had
no sense that the official language was changing. He preserved Chaucer's
dichotomy between the languages of his professional writing and the
language of his poetry.

   We have no descriptions of the pedagogical methods of the writing
masters who taught *ars dictaminis* in Chaucer's time, but the statutes of
the Rivington grammar school ("grammar school" meant Latin grammar and composition until the eighteenth century) 150 years later specify:

   divising and writing sundry epistles, to sundry persons, of sundry
   matters, as of chiding, exhorting, comforting, counselling, praying,
   lamenting; some to friends, some to foes, some to strangers; of
   weighty matters, or merry, as shooting, hunting, etc.; of adversity, of
   prosperity, of war and peace, divine and profane, of all sciences and
   occupations, some long, some short.[38]

This syllabus could be a description of the contents of the *Canterbury Tales*. Chaucer's education in *ars dictaminis* must have been much like it: imitating the formulary models in learning to write sundry letters to sundry individuals on sundry topics, each in its appropriate style. This had been the mode of clerical training for centuries, but Chaucer was the first to take the imaginative step from creating letters in different registers to imagining the composers speaking their letters in their own voices.

The imaginative step was involved with the emergence of the sense of the individual in Chaucer's poetry, which we will examine in the next chapter. The point to be made here is that this important contribution that Chaucer made to the evolution of English literature grew out of his clerical training in the inns of chancery. His *Canterbury Tales* can be regarded simply as a dramatized formulary.

A final comment on Chaucer's prose before we turn to the emergence of the individual. The Parson's Tale in the Canterbury collection shows Chaucer's mastery of the homiletic style which R. W. Chambers claimed provided the continuity between Anglo-Saxon and Modern English prose.[39] This prose was in the first instance directed towards women and others who did not know French—specifically not the Anglo-Norman aristocracy. Recent critics express doubts about Chambers's thesis, and maintain that Modern English prose was recreated in the fifteenth and sixteenth centuries chiefly through translation and adaptation of French and Latin.[40] If that is the case, Chaucer is a precursor here, too, because his *Boece* and *Tale of Melibee* are translations of French translations from Latin. Although Chaucer had been educated in Latin and had to use Latin regularly in his custom house accounting (Latin continued as the language of the exchequer long after the other offices of government had switched to English; entries in the Pells accounts of the Exchequer of Receipts were made in Latin until this file came to an end on 10 October 1834, at which point someone wrote in pencil "Diem mortis Saccari"—"the day of the death of the Exchequer"), he never translated without a French pony. For *Boece* he worked from the French translation of Jean de Meun but emended from the Latin, but for *Melibee* he evidently knew only the French translation by Renaud de Louens. The closest parallels to the Parson's Tale are all Latin, but its style is so French that it is likely that the French original simply has not yet turned up. It has been suggested that these pieces might have been commissioned by King Richard's mother, Joan of Kent, as texts to help with the education of the young king.[41] But this assumes that Richard's education would have been in English, which is highly unlikely. It is much more probable that Ralph Strode, John Gower, Thomas Usk, and other inns of court associates provided the audience for these experiments in expository English than members of the royal household—although, again, we must not imagine that the court and the city were completely separate audiences. Sir Richard Stury, Sir Lewis Clifford, Simon Burley, and others, like Chaucer himself, were closely associated with both the court and the bureaucracy, and there must have been entertainments like those at the inns of court and merchant puis (which we will discuss in chapter 4) attended by both bodies. It is hard to distinguish between a courtly and a civic audience for moral and political essays. These would have been of interest to anyone concerned with the government during the bad rule of Richard II that culminated in his overthrow by Henry IV.

Chaucer's other prose was directed to a much more specialized audience. The *Treatise on the Astrolabe* has been called the first competent work on astronomy in English.[42] In order to justify its being in English, Chaucer addressed it to "Litell Lewis my sone," which titillated the biographers (was "Lewis" Lewis Clifford's son; was he the result of the rape of Cecily Champain?) until J. M. Manly turned up a record of a Lewis Chaucer associated with Thomas Chaucer, both of whom he took to be the sons of the poet.[43] At least we may conclude that this essay was not directed to an aristocratic patron, but represents another experiment by Chaucer in tackling a formidable subject in English for a bourgeois audience. The same thing must be true of what is now generally accepted as our only Chaucer holograph—that is, a manuscript in his own hand—*Equatorie of the Planets*. This is an even more mathematically accomplished compilation of star tables and instructions as to how to construct and use an instrument for calculating the positions of the heavenly bodies. It was obviously in the process of composition when it was laid aside, and recent scholars have concluded that it is indeed by Chaucer, which means that the manuscript gives us a sample of Chaucer's own handwriting, language, and method of composition.[44]

There is the question of how Chaucer was introduced to the highly technical field of astronomy. Most of his immediate sources are Latin translations from Arabic, but there is an extensive literature in French with which one presumes he would have been acquainted. John North in *Chaucer's Universe* says that his allusions to the Aristotelian universe are not the sort that indicate a university education. But Ralph Strode, his possible companion in law school, had been a fellow of Merton College, Oxford, the fourteenth-century English center of astronomical calculation. It could have been with Strode's help that he began the studies that led to those "products of the Oxford school," the *Astrolabe* and the *Equatorie*. The progress from casual astronomical observations in his early poems to systematic horoscopes in his later poems and then to the calculations in the treatises show his growing interest and proficiency in the subject, until he evidently laid aside his poetry in his retirement and devoted himself to full-time study of astronomy. The pervasiveness of astronomical allegory and dating that North identifies in Chaucer's poems (more, it must be admitted, than the average reader will care to accept) led him to suggest that Chaucer must have had a circle of friends in the 1380s knowledgeable enough about the details of astronomy, astrology, geomancy, and other scientific phenomena to appreciate the complexity of his allusions and his efforts to write about such technical matters in their native language. Be this as it may, the present argument is that his audience would have been composed not of members of the court but of educated bureaucrats and merchants like

Ralph Strode and John Gower. The philosophical and scientific aspects of his writing represent a further extension of English to express the concerns of the civic dimension of society.

In the first chapter we traced Chaucer's part in bringing prestige to a language that had for three hundred years been a plebian patois. Prestige in language grows out of the power and influence of those who use it and the uses to which it is put. As long as the English aristocracy spoke French and wrote in French for government, commerce, and culture, English remained a patois. By 1350, the Anglo-Norman aristocrats, having lost the Norman property that made them French, were beginning to think of themselves as English. Their continued rule over Aquitaine was military; they did not have the sort of personal investment there that they had had in Normandy. The domestic language of the majority of the population began to become the domestic language of the aristocracy. By the time of Henry V it would begin to become the language of government and commerce. In the meantime, poets writing in English began to make it the language of culture. Chaucer, educated both in the royal courts and the inns of court, was the most visible and most gifted writer to express in English the refinement and sophistication hitherto considered possible only in French. Chaucer was not the only writer making this transition. The poems of the *Gawain and the Green Knight* poet were just as sophisticated as anything by Chaucer. But that writer was not of the London court and wrote in a provincial dialect. Chaucer's brilliant achievement in the court dialect ennobled English to the point where other writers for the aristocracy, especially his friend John Gower, could begin to use it for cultivated literature. Chaucer gave English prestige, albeit a prestige at first perhaps clouded by his domestic situation. But Prince Henry was soon to take care of that, as we shall see in the last chapter.

Prestige was only the first of Chaucer's contributions. In this second chapter we have traced the emergence of the educated middle class so well documented by Paul Strohm[45] which would in succeeding centuries take charge of all aspects of English culture. Chaucer, born into and educated in this class, was the first writer to address its spiritual, philo-sophical, moral, civic, economic, and scientific concerns. Again, he was not alone. The author of *Piers Plowman* dealt with many of the same spiritual and social concerns, and scholars like John Trevisa were begin-ning to translate history and science from Latin into English. But they had no connection with the culture of either the royal courts or the inns of court, and Langland, at least, wrote in a provincial dialect. Chaucer ennobled English, but he also broadened it by showing its adequacy for sophisticated discourse, and particularly for mimesis—the representa-tion of reality through language.

We turn next to Chaucer's third major contribution, the emergence of awareness of the individual self in English writing. Again, the self was not Chaucer's invention. He was transmuting what scholastic writers in Latin and vernacular writers in French and Italian had been developing for two centuries. But Chaucer was the first to express it in English.

3.

Chaucer and the Emergence of the Individual

Chaucer was the first English person to emerge as an "author." There are others whose names we know, beginning with Caedmon and Layamon and continuing through Chaucer's contemporaries like John Gower and William Langland, but these are shadowy figures who seem merely to reinforce the anonymity of the creator in medieval culture. Only heroes and saints emerge with anything like personalities in the early Middle Ages—Charlemagne, Alfred the Great, Richard the Lion-Hearted, or St. Antony, St. Augustine, St. Francis.

The medieval view of society was strictly corporate.[1] Its concept of the community was the *corpus Christi,* described by St. Paul in I Corinthians 12:12. As with the human body, each of the community's members had a specific function, without which the whole could not survive. This platonic view of community is by definition hierarchic and totalitarian. The head directs the hands and feet, which in turn sustain the head. The organism and its functions are created and sustained by God, not, as in the eighteenth-century social contract, by the consent of its members. Only the head, the ruler, was called upon to make decisions. The other members were absorbed into the commune and existed only through their functions. Who were the medieval craftsmen, the merchants? Who were the architects of the cathedrals, the composers of the music, the painters, the poets? There are hagiographies but no biographies. There are no portraits. Until the letters of Abelard and Heloise, Dante, and Petrarch, there are no diaries, no personal correspondence.

Chaucer was instrumental in ushering into English literature a new perception of the importance of the individual. Again, it took time for this to become self-conscious, but the life of Chaucer in Speght's edition (1598) is the first biography in English of a British author. John Leland's *Commentarie de Scriptoribus Britannicis* (c. 1550), the first collection of British authors' lives, from which Speght and other commentators drew, was in Latin, and not printed until 1709. The apparatus of Speght's edition of Chaucer is the first in which an English author is treated as a classic. And Francis Thynne's criticism of the edition, "Animadversions vppon the Annotacions and Corrections of some imperfections of impressiones of Chaucers workes" (1598), is the first scholarship on English literature.[2]

As awareness of Chaucer as an author grew, so did awareness of his mimology (the belief that there must be a relation between the word and the thing[3]). We will trace the development of this awareness in the last chapter, but it was quite self-conscious by the time of Dryden's observation in the preface to his *Fables* (1700) that Chaucer "has taken into the Compass of the *Canterbury Tales* the various Manners and Humours of the whole English nation. . . . Not a single character has escaped him," and Blake's (1809) that the General Prologue presents the "lineaments of universal human life. . . . As Newton numbered the stars, and Linneus numbered the plants, Chaucer numbered the classes of men."[4]

In this chapter I want to explore the background and nature of Chaucer's own sense of authorship and of his characters as individual personalities. Awareness of authorship and individualism had been vivid in classical literature but had virtually disappeared from the sixth to the eleventh centuries. It began to reappear in what has been called the renaissance of the twelfth century. How aware Chaucer was of the learned background it is hard to say, but awareness of the emergence of the individual in the fourteenth century must have been akin to our awareness of the emergence of the unconscious in the twentieth—neither authors nor audiences need to have read Nietzsche or Freud to be aware of the psyche. It is in the air.

Awareness of the creator as an individual grew out of the improvement of education beginning in the eleventh century.[5] During the Dark Ages from the sixth century until the eleventh, most written materials appeared to the minority who could read as an undifferentiated gestalt emanating from impersonal authority, like the pyramids or other ancient monuments. There were no title pages indicating author and publisher. Texts were not divided into sections. There were no tables of contents or indexes. The Bible served as a prototype for all writing. Latin *scriptura* meant simply "writing," and until the fifteenth century the English usage was largely neutral; Chaucer's four uses of the term are all neutral, meaning simply the written record, as when the narrator in *Legend of Good Women* refers to "Eneas—but as of that scripture, / Be as be may" (3.1144). When it referred to the Bible, scripture was modified by "holy." By 1600, however, "scripture" without the modifier had come to be restricted largely to the Bible, which the *Oxford English Dictionary* gives as its priority meaning today.

The Scriptures as an unanalyzed mass were the Word of God. God was the *auctor,* which in Latin meant "authority." Pope Gregory compared the human writers of the books of the Bible to pens. We do not ask with what pen an *auctor* composes, so we do not ask who was the author of Job.[6] The Bible was not divided into chapters until the thirteenth century, nor into verses until the sixteenth. Verses in the Old Testament were indicated in the Hebrew manuscripts of the Talmud, but were not used in the medieval Vulgate. Hugh of St. Cher (d. 1263), in the first alphabetical concordance to the Bible, divided the chapters into seven sections, designated A–G. Verses were not numbered until in the Vulgate printed by Henry Stephens in 1555. Henry's father Robert had first divided the New Testament into verses on a horseback trip from Paris to Lyons for a Greek-Latin edition he published in 1551.[7]

The dividing and classifying of the Scriptures epitomized the growth of literary awareness that authors and editors could manipulate the text. Until the text began to be looked at in this way, there could be no sense of "a creator," but only of "The Creator." Texts were simply extrapolations of the *auctor* in the original sense of the word. Only an ancient could be an authority. But as schools and universities came into being and command of Latin improved, manuscripts and commentaries began to be compared and students became aware of differences in texts and styles. The scholastics began to distinguish between the functions of auctor, scriptor, compilator, and commentator.

The rediscovery of Aristotle in the thirteenth century introduced the concept of causality—the idea that the universe was not merely a static manifestation of the will of God, but subject to temporal change and human influence.[8] In the world of nature this perception gave rise to the experimental science of Roger Bacon and Robert Grosseteste. In the world of philosophy, it led to the identification of four kinds of causes: the efficient cause, the creator; the material cause, the creation; the formal cause, the method of creation; and the final cause, the purpose or intention of the creation. Although such pedantic analysis has given scholasticism a bad name, its painstaking procedures for identifying and classifying the elements of a concept, either concrete or abstract, are the foundations of Western learning, the essential meaning of "sophistication": the capacity to look at an object or a subject and discern its constituent parts; at a coat and discern its material, its sleeves, and its collar; at a landscape and discern hills, valleys, and streams; at love and discern physical, emotional, and social constituents. Inability to make such distinctions is what we call naiveté.

In literature, Aristotle's theory of causality helped to bring about awareness of the personal author in contrast to the impersonal authority. Biblical criticism ("criticism" is derived from Greek *kritikos*, meaning ability to divide and classify) began to distinguish different principles and styles in different parts of the Bible, and thence between God as the authority for the whole and human writers as the authors of the parts. This led to extensive discussion of the *forma tractandi*, the method of composition, and the *forma tractatus,* the organization of the material, and of the *causa effective librorum,* the author as the creator of the book, and *causa movens scriptorum,* the purpose or occasion that moves the author to write. The scholastic *accessus,* or introduction to the study of an ancient text, came to be structured about "who, what, why, where, when, whence, and in what manner," very nearly the elements still treated in the headnote to a modern school edition.[9]

Aristotle's *Categories* and *Analytics* had been known to the Roman writers like Cicero and Boethius, and their discussion of authorial freedom of selection in style and organization of materials provided a cogent example for the scholastics. But until the fourteenth century, pagan authors were regarded with great suspicion, and even in Chaucer's time a medieval fundamentalist like John Wyclif still could denounce sophisticated literary analysis of scriptural styles and authors as blasphemous.[10] The Bible was the Word of God, all of a piece, as it is to many people still. Nevertheless, the awareness of ancient authors and rhetoricians about styles and genres and authorial control provided insights and language by which to describe the styles and genres of the Bible, and by the fourteenth century scriptural and pagan *auctores* had come together in terms of literary analysis. Preachers could appeal to classical examples in their sermons,[11] paving the way for poets like Machaut and Chaucer to weave classical and Christian language and imagery together in their secular poetry.

Thirteenth-century commentators like Thomas Aquinas began to show awareness of the personalities of the authors of the Scriptures as they discussed the different intentions and audiences for the epistles of Paul, or the different genres Solomon employed in Proverbs and the Song of Solomon, or whether all of the Psalms were by David. Out of this grew the conviction that the thought of an author could be best understood in the context of his work as a whole, and so began the compilation of *originalia,* anthologies of all of the works of authorities like St. Augustine or St. Bernard, and collections of lives of both Christian and pagan authors deduced from their writings.

The emerging scholastic awareness of authorship was paralleled by the emerging voice of the author in twelfth- and thirteenth-century secular poetry. Classical poets like Ovid and Horace had been very personal in their expression, as had prose writers like St. Augustine and Boethius. But such personal sentiments as "I think" or "it seems to me" and poetry and prose expressing the personal joys and fears of the writer largely disappeared in the Dark Ages. They reappeared in the troubadour poems of Provence, the poems of Marie de France, the goliardic poems, and such an autobiographical collection, nearly unique in its time, as Peter Abelard's *Historia Calamitatum* (c. 1135), and became an important aspect of the poetry and prose of the thirteenth and fourteenth centuries.[12]

It is hard to believe that there has ever been a culture lacking first person lyrical expression; such expression is crucial to human self-consciousness. A truism of psycholinguistics is that until a sentiment is expressed in language it cannot be felt. The Greek and Roman lyric and elegiac poets had expressed the gamut of sentiments in their native languages. The problem is that from about A.D. 500 to about 1000, imperial Latin was the only form of writing, long after it had ceased to be the native language of most of the writers. One seldom utters endearments or complaints in a foreign language. People no doubt continued to brood over their personal joys and griefs, but in dialects seldom preserved in writing. A few early lyrics like the Anglo-Saxon "Wife's Lament" and "Husband's Message," and "Wanderer" and "Seafarer," are preserved from this oral period. But very soon after the vernacular dialects began to be written down, we find the rebirth of first-person lyrical expression. The history of European literature traces this rebirth to the troubadour songs because a continuity can be traced from them as it cannot from the Anglo-Saxon.

There is a library of argument as to the extent to which this first-person mode is an assertion of the individual. One influential body of scholars finds it largely rhetorical, an aspect of the evolution of literature from recitation to reading.[13] They point out that communication always implies establishment of a relationship between sender and receiver. On the part of the sender: Just how am I going to couch this statement? What language am I going to use? On the part of the receiver: What does he or she mean? Am I pleased or put off by the manner of expression? The sender must adopt a mask appropriate to the situation. Under the best of circumstances, the receiver will understand the mask and adopt a reciprocal mask to receive the message. The mask assumed by the sender instructs the receiver as to how he or she should react: cooperatively or uncooperatively. This matching of masks is what we call empathy. The masks of epic poems intended for recitation are quite straightforward. The narrative is impersonal and objective. The author is omniscient. He never editorializes, never expresses approval, disapproval, certainty, doubt. The poetic "I" never appears. There is no ambiguity about actions or motives. The audience is always informed directly, as with Unferth in *Beowulf*: "He released his hostile words; Beowulf's venture, spirited seafaring, displeased him greatly, for he grudged that any other man in the middle earth should win more glory than he" (501–505). The paralinguistics of the teller—his tone of voice, gestures, and facial expressions—instruct the audience as to how they should react to what is being told. And the audience responds as a group, exhilarated or angered by group psychology. This was the rhetoric of expository communication from about A.D. 500 until after 1000 as it still is today.

But with the rebirth of written communication, the rhetorical situation shifted. Unlike recitation to an audience, reading is a solitary activity that implies a one-to-one relationship between the sender and receiver. Every successful writer—like every successful television anchor—must learn how to achieve this intimacy with the individual reader. From the twelfth century on, as solitary reading increased, the author could less and less count on governance by the paralinguistics of the reciter and had to begin to create other devices to instruct the reader how to react—what mask to assume.

The reappearance of the "I" in literature must have been a combination of these impulses: the participatory "I" of the speaker expressing personal sentiments, and the editorial "I" of the writer instructing the reader how to respond to the message. Exploring the ramifications of the two voices through the vernacular and Latin literature of the high Middle Ages is a rewarding enterprise, and we shall have more to say about them when we discuss the Chaucerian voices in the next chapter. But we must now return to the part they play in the emergence of the idea of the author and of the individual. By the fourteenth century, scholastic critics were aware of scriptural and classical writers as authors/ creators who spoke with different voices on different occasions, but such awareness emerged only gradually with regard to modern vernacular authors. Dante (1265–1321) was one of the first to regard himself in this way, when he composed *Vita Nuova* to provide a context for Provençal-type lyrics he had composed at random over a number of years and as a prologue to *Divine Comedy,* and by the integrity of the personality presented in his poems and his prose works. The participatory "I" creates the personality that we come to recognize as Dante the writer and persuades us that it voices deeply felt personal emotions as in the troubadour lyrics or any other autobiographical expressions. But the observations of the editorial "I" direct the reader how he or she should react to the experiences of romantic and spiritual love in the figure of Beatrice or to the mimetic personalities in Hell, Purgatory, and Heaven. Dante projected the first image of an author in medieval times. The personal style of the *Vita Nuova, Divine Comedy, Convivio,* and *Letter to the Con Grande* was more self-exegetical than any writing since classical times. Dante is the first writer to leave a corpus of letters explaining his intentions and sentiments. No matter whether the "I" of his writings was autobiographical or editorial, it created a literary personality seized upon at once by his contemporaries. The first commentary on the *Divine Comedy*—the earliest upon any post-classical poem—was written by Graziolo de' Bambaglioli in 1324, just three years after Dante's death, and there were two other commentaries composed before 1340.

Boccaccio was lecturing on Dante in Florence when Chaucer was there in 1373; his early lectures were the earliest biographical recognition of a modern poet, and the later lectures began to explicate the *Inferno* as a classic, until they were cut off by his death. Petrarch was in Padua at the time of Chaucer's visit to Genoa and Florence in 1373. There has always been the tantalizing question of whether Chaucer got to hear Boccaccio and meet Petrarch on this trip. We have no evidence, but Dante and Petrarch are the only contemporary poets Chaucer ever names, so their emergence as authors must have influenced his conception of himself. Chaucer cites Dante in *House of Fame,* in which he characterizes himself most specifically, in *Legend of Good Women* (twice), and in the Knight's Tale, Wife of Bath's prologue, and Friar's Tale in the Canterbury collection. He cites Petrarch twice as the author of the Clerk's Tale of the patient Griselda, and as the author of Zenobia in the Monk's Tale. Both of these stories are actually by Boccaccio; his failure ever to acknowledge his many borrowings from Boccaccio is one of Chaucer's most intriguing silences.

After Dante, Petrarch (1304–1374) emerges as the most striking literary personality in the Middle Ages. Indeed, Petrarch quickly overshadowed Dante because of his contributions to the rise of humanism. But it is Petrarch's self-awareness as an author and his attention to the inner workings of the human psyche that may have reinforced Chaucer's sensitivity to the same concerns, which tend much more toward Petrarch's and Boccaccio's psychological view of personality than toward Dante's spiritual view or Machaut's chivalric view. Petrarch began his famous "Letter to Posterity":

> You may perhaps have heard something about me—although it is
> doubtful that my poor little name may travel far in space and time.
> Still, you may by chance want to know what sort of man I was or
> what was the fate of my works, especially of those whose reputation
> may have persisted, or whose name you may have vaguely heard.[14]

Among the many classical manuscripts that Petrarch "recovered" were the collections of Cicero's and Pliny's personal letters. From these he conceived the idea of composing similar letters that record his contributions to the rise of humanism. They include personal reminiscences and comments on authorship, book collecting, antiquity, recovery of classical manuscripts, fame, fortune, friendship, and all of the other subjects that would become important to Renaissance humanists. Although some of the letters were actually sent to contemporary addressees, many were addressed to dead authors like Cicero, Seneca, Virgil, and Homer, and all were written for preservation as literary works. These letters, even more than Dante's, provide a basis for literary biography. Just as Boccaccio had provided the first biography of Dante in his Florence lectures, he wrote the first biography of Petrarch, *De vita et moribus domini Francisci Petracchi de Florentia* (1341).

Although Petrarch provided the Renaissance archetype for the ideas of author and authorship, he sent mixed signals about the value of the vernacular language. All of his essays and letters and what he considered to be his most important poems are in Latin. This is the other face of what we call humanism. It was on the one hand the transfer to the vernacular of writing for commerce and government, but on the other the polishing of Latin for literature and learning. The Italian *Canzonieri*, 366 lyrics on Petrarch's love for Madonna Laura, 317 of them in the sonnet form that had such influence on later poetry, Petrarch himself called "trifles." This was a pose, because he labored over these poems for thirty years as we can tell from the work sheets that have been preserved. But his display of Latin and demurral about Italian exhibit the same sort of distrust of literature in the vernacular that Chaucer must have faced in London.

However, Dante, Boccaccio, and Petrarch may have focused the concept of vernacular authorship in the fourteenth century, it must have been Guillaume de Machaut who provided for Chaucer the most immediate models of the author and the book—author in the medieval sense of a writer who is supported by patrons for his writing, not a bureaucrat like Deschamps or Chaucer whose writing was incidental to responsible and onerous clerical service, and book in the sense of a work to be read by the solitary reader, not a libretto to be heard by an audience. Dante began as a civic officer in Florence, but after his party fell from power in 1302, he lived out the rest of his life supported by powerful patrons in Verona, Ravenna, and elsewhere. Boccaccio was the first professional hack, in contrast to Dante's being the first professional author. As a boy Boccaccio worked in the banking firm of his father, who supported him until his father went bankrupt in 1345. After that, Boccaccio lived by ad hoc commissions for copying manuscripts and writing and lecturing, as when the Signoria of Florence commissioned him just before his death to lecture on Dante for a fee of a hundred florins. Machaut had a career more like Dante's. For a dozen years he may have served as secretary to King Jean of Luxemburg, but in his middle thirties (1337) he was granted an honorary canonry at the cathedral of Rheims. From that time on he lived there composing music and writing poetry, which he dedicated to a series of Luxemburg and French royal patrons, as Petrarch had done from Vaucluse, and Dante from Verona and Ravenna.

Machaut frequently refers to himself as an author and to his poems as compositions to be read,[15] but his *Livre dou voir dit* (Book of the true story), completed about 1364 near the beginning of Chaucer's own career, is his most remarkable presentation of himself as an author.[16] Modeled in a general way upon Abelard's *Historia Calamitatum* and Dante's *Vita Nuova*, it tells of a love affair between an aging poet and a young woman who falls in love with him through reading his poems and initiates a correspondence. The work includes the prose letters they exchanged and many lyrics. In both, Machaut speaks of his literary intentions, methods of composition, principles of organizing and compiling his works, and the responses he anticipates from the lady, Toute Belle, and other readers. Sometimes he addresses the reader directly, explaining the strategy of a letter. At one point (7719–8160), when he puts the lady's picture in a drawer because he suspects that she has been unfaithful, the picture tells him in a dream the Ovidian story of how the crow turned black that Chaucer used as the Manciple's Tale in the Canterbury collection.

Machaut's *Voir dit* provides an important transition between the participatory and editorial voices. The author begins as a lover speaking of his emotional involvement with Toute Belle and gradually shifts to the voice of the writer speaking about the composition and organization of his poems. Chaucer's friend John Gower represents something of the same transition in *Confessio Amantis,* beginning as a lover and ending as the "moral Gower" who is too old to be a lover and has completed the collection of poems assigned him by the king, and is advising Chaucer to complete the collection assigned him by Alceste.[17] The same transition marks the development of Chaucer's own self-presentation as an author. At the beginning of his career, in *Book of the Duchess,* the narrator cannot fall asleep for love,

> a sicknesse
> That I have suffred this eight yeere—
> And yet my boote [remedy] is never the nere [nearer],
> For there is phisicien but oon
> That may me hele [heal].
>
> (*BD* 36–40)

In *Parliament of Fowls* he begins with a reference to his writing, "The lyf so short, the craft so long to lerne," and goes on to say:

> For al be that I knowe nat Love in dede,
> Ne wot [know] how that he quiteth [pays] folk her hyre
> [their wages].
>
> (*PF* 8–9)

And in *House of Fame,* Jove sends him the eagle to take him to learn about love because "thou hast no tydynges / Of Loves folk . . . / And lyvest thus as an heremyte" (*HF* 644, 659). This transformation from the participatory voice of the lover into the editorial voice of the narrator grows even more marked in *Troylus and Criseyde* and *Canterbury Tales.*

The question of how Chaucer envisaged his poems being received is moot. In the era before books and radio and television, oral entertain-

ment of one kind or another was the most common way to while away
the time, and it has been commonly assumed that Chaucer intended his
poetry for oral recitation. Address to the hearer is frequent. In virtually
every one of his poems, something like two hundred times, he asks his
audience to "hear" his poetry, in phrases like:

> And seyde hem thus, as ye shul after here.
>
> (PF 658)

> Pray I that he wol me spede
> My swevene [dream] for to telle aryght . . .
> So yive hem joye that hyt here.
>
> (HF 78–83)

> And preyeth for hem that ben yn the cas
> Of Troylus, as ye may after here . . .
>
> (TC 1.29–30)

> And certes, if it nere [were not] to long to heere,
> I wolde yow have toold . . .
>
> (CT 1.875–76)

In contrast, most of the 135 occurrences of "read" refer to Chaucer's own
reading of his sources or other allusions to reading within the poems,
as at the beginning of *Book of the Duchess*:

> So when I saw I might not slepe
> Til now late this other night,
> Upon my bedde I sat upright
> And bad oon [someone] reche me a booke,
> A romaunce, and he it me toke,
> To rede and drive the night away.
>
> (BD 44–49)

But it is quite clear that Chaucer thought of his poems as being
read, and that he thought of his works as books. The most familiar

reference to reading is in the prologue to the Miller's Tale, where he defends himself for writing a bawdy story:

> I moot reherce
> Hir [their] tales alle, be they bettre or werse,
> Or elles falsen som of my mateere.
> And therfore, whoso list it nat yheere,
> Turne over the leef and chese another tale.
>
> (*CT* 1.3173–77)

Turning over the leaf implies that he envisages the poem as a book, but "yheere" implies that the book was being heard. The explanation is that until after the advent of printing reading even to oneself was assumed to be oral. The Latin term *lectura* meant reading. French *lecture* still means reading, as it did in Middle English. But as silent reading developed, the oral dimension of "lecture" prevailed, giving rise to the present sense of "public address," first recorded in the *OED* in 1536.

A memorable cameo in the *Confessions* of St. Augustine is his description of St. Ambrose reading to himself: "Now, as he read, his eyes glanced over the pages and his heart searched out the sense, but his voice and tongue were silent."[18] Augustine, professor of rhetoric and prolific author, had never seen a person reading silently before. The three hours a day prescribed in the Benedictine Rule for *lectio divina* were understood to be oral reading. Indeed, when the Cluniac monks instituted the vow of silence, they had to drastically reduce the period for *lectio*.[19]

The same is true of secular reading. In the mid-fifteenth-century romance *Eger and Grime:*

> Into a window Sir Egar yeede [went]
> Bookes of romans [romances] for to reede
> That all the court might hem [them] heare.
>
> (627–29)

And we recall the charming scene in *Troylus and Criseyde* when Pandarus comes to Criseyde's palace:

> And fond [found] two othere ladyes sette, and she,
> Withinne a paved parlour, and thei thre
> Herden a mayden reden hem the geste [epic]
> Of the sege of Thebes.
>
> (*TC* 2.81–84)

So Chaucer's references to "hearing" his poems is compatible with the notion that he composed them as texts to be read aloud whether by the solitary reader or to a group. This is confirmed by his famous entreaty at the end of *Troylus and Criseyde:*

> Go litel bok, go litel myn tragedye,
> Ther [to where, "and may"] God thi makere yet, er
>   that he dye,
> So sende myght to make yn [compose] som comedye.
> But litel bok, no makyng thow n'envye,
> But subgit [subject] be to alle poesye,
> And kys the steppes where as thow seest pace [walk]
> Virgile, Ovyde, Omer [Homer], Lukan, and Stace
>   [Statius].
>
> And for ther is so gret dyversite
> In Englyssh and yn wrytyng of oure tonge,
> So prey I God that noon myswryte thee,
> Ne thee mysmetre for defaute [default] of tonge.
> And red wherso thow be, or elles songe,
> That thow be understonde, God I beseche—
>
> (*TC* 5.1786–98)

This reveals Chaucer's conception of himself as the author of a written text who is concerned about how the audience will receive his message.[20]

Of course, reading for information and entertainment was only one kind of reading, and after the tenth century, when study of written texts began to supplement narrative reading, the oral nature of the process grew less pronounced.[21] Lists, tables, glosses, and figures that had to be compared and contrasted could not be consulted orally. The evolution of scholastic philosophy and science called more and more for silent cogitation over the written symbols. However he may have thought his poetry would be aprehended, Chaucer's technical prose was set down with the silent reader in mind. The figures that accompany the propositions in *Treatise on the Astrolabe* and *Equatorie of the Planets,* in the latter certainly by the author himself, are strictly visual communication.[22]

Silent reading encouraged the enlargement of the realm of private experience, indulgence in fantasies and epiphanies that would be repressed in public expression. It fostered the growth of the private religious experience so characteristic of the later Middle Ages. It encouraged a more cynical and ironic view of the world outside, as reflected in Deschamps, Chaucer, and Villon. It stimulated revival of erotic art and frank sexual language. The "heigh fantesye" (*CT* 4.1577) of old January in Chaucer's Merchant's Tale, lying in his bed, hallucinating about the pretty girls in the neighborhood, is eerily prescient of Freudian psychology. Chaucer's fabliaux and prologue to the Wife of Bath's Tale may indeed have been enjoyed in public performance, but generations of silent readers since 1400 have found that as written texts they can be explored and savored in so many different ways. The persona of the oral presenter appears to control Chaucer's poetry, but it is only careful study of the written text that reveals the full dimension of his expression.

Chaucer's self-awareness as an author is further evidenced by the fact that he is the first English author to recognize his own productions as an oeuvre. In contemporary criticism, "oeuvre" implies the sum total of an author's production. As we said above, one of the perceptions of scholastic criticism was that an author's meaning could best be understood in the context of his complete works, which led to compilation of collections of the *originalia*. Petrarch compiled carefully organized collections of his letters. Guillaume de Machaut compiled several elaborate manuscripts of his complete works. Eustache Deschamps made at least one carefully organized collection of his poems. Chaucer twice gives lists of his works. The first, in the prologue to *Legend of Good Women,* is couched as a defense against the accusation that he had "spoken against women" by portraying the falsity of Criseyde (F440–41). Evidently, as we shall see, the psychological realism and satire towards which his poetry was tending in *Parliament of Fowls, House of Fame,* and *Troylus* must have perturbed conservatives who expected traditional treatments of courtly love and had been pleased by the ennoblement of English in *Book of the Duchess.* This defense in *Legend of Good Women* was written before he had conceived the fabilaux in *Canterbury Tales,* which, of course, went even further than *Troylus* towards satire and naturalism.

In the retraction at the end of the *Canterbury Tales,* Chaucer gives another list of his writings in which his awareness of the authorial dilemma is very clear. It is addressed "to hem all that herkne this litel tretys [*Canterbury Tales*] or rede," and to readers whose reactions have to be directed by signals furnished by the absent writer. "And if ther be anythyng that displese hem," he continues, "I preye hem also that they arrette [ascribe] it to the defaute of myn unkonnynge [lack of skill], and nat to my wyl that wolde ful fayn have seyd bettre if I hadde had konnynge" (10.1082–83). He retracts all of his poems, including *Book of the Duchess* and *Tales of Caunterbury,* "thilke [those] that sownen into [tend towards] sin" (10.1086), and vindicates himself by *Boece* "and othere bookes of legendes of seintes, and omelies, and moralitee, and devocioun" (10.1087). This is the authorial persona Chaucer projected into the fifteenth century—the image of the writer concerned about the way his writings would be received by future readers, and aware that he could no longer be sure of the responses once they had been launched.

This image brings us back to the enigma on which we have commented before in connection with Chaucer's silences. The Chaucer who twice gave lists of his oeuvre and commended his books to posterity at the end of his two principal works, *Troylus and Criseyde* and *Canterbury Tales,* is the Chaucer who died leaving behind him not only no collection of his works but evidently not one finished manuscript of any single work. Nearly all Chaucer scholars attribute this deficiency to the fortune of his manuscripts. It is true that many more manuscripts have been lost from the Middle Ages than have been preserved. So few can be traced to exact exemplars (that is, copy texts from which the scribe worked) that it is cliché that there are one or more manuscripts lost for every one that has come down. But this cliché is not applicable to the case of Chaucer. In the era before printing, presentation to a patron was the customary way to publish and receive remuneration for one's writings. We can observe this process in the fine presentation manuscripts that have been preserved from other court poets like Machaut, Deschamps, Froissart, and even a poet as distantly associated with the court as Chaucer's friend John Gower. Even though most of Chaucer's poems may have been intended for a bourgeois audience, it is inconceivable that if he or his admirers were concerned about the preservation of his poems, there would be no presentation manuscripts of works clearly directed to royal patrons such as *Book of the Duchess* and *Legend of Good Women*. Chaucer had access to professional copiests. John Shirley, who copied and preserved so many of his short poems, has a delightful expostulation headed "Chauciers wordes. Geffrey unto Adame his owen scryveyne [scrivener, professional copiest, what we would today call typist]":

> Adam scryveyn, if ever it thee byfalle
> *Boece* or *Troylus* for to wryten newe,
> Under thy long lokkes thow most have the scalle [itch]
> But after my makyng [composing] thow wryte more trewe!
> So ofte a daye I mot thy werk renewe
> It to corecte and eke to rubbe and scrape;
> And al is thorugh thy neglygence and rape![23]

What is it that Adam was copying if it was not presentation manu-scripts of some kind? Since no such manuscript has come down, it appears that he was merely making fair copies for Chaucer himself, and that Chaucer deliberately withheld them from circulation during his lifetime. Why? The reasons could have been both personal and sociolin-guistic. On the personal side, we have the evidence that not one of the 493 life records recording Chaucer's public life ever mentions him as an author, which indicates how unimportant this activity must have seemed both to him and to his contemporaries. On the sociolinguistic side, the lack of manuscripts before 1400 supports the notion that as much as we see Chaucer's production as the fountainhead of English literature, during his lifetime it was looked upon askance, as a curiosity rather than as an achievement.

This explanation is also fraught with problems. It is obvious that before 1386 Deschamps in France knew of a translation of *Roman de la Rose* that has not come down to us, and that before 1388 Thomas Usk in his *Testament of Love* could quote extensively from *Boece* and adapt lines from *House of Fame, Troylus,* and *Legend of Good Women*.[24] And by 1400 Chaucer must have achieved notoriety as evidenced by the rapid appearance of the manuscripts and allusions that we will discuss in the last chapter. So Chaucer's models of literary English—that is, English intended to be read, not merely heard—and his reputation as a vernacular author were somehow being disseminated during the last two decades of the fourteenth century in spite of the lack of any manuscripts deemed worthy of preservation.

The precedence of Chaucer as the image of an author raises further problems because Chaucer never gives us an autobiographical account of authorship like Gower's description of his meeting with the king on the royal barge at the beginning of *Confessio Amantis,* or Machaut's of his visit to the dauphin's court in *Voir dit.* The political discussion between the dauphin and Machaut could have suggested to Chaucer the political discussion between Alceste and the poet in *Legend of Good Women,* but, if so, it dramatically demonstrates the difference between Machaut's autobiographical mode and Chaucer's allegorical transformation. Petrarch, Machaut, Deschamps, and Froissart throughout their writings describe in detail their experiences with patrons and readers, so Chaucer must have been familiar with the mode. He simply chose not to use it. The closest he comes is in the prologue to *Treatise on the Astrolabe* where he describes his intentions of writing in English for "litell Lowys my sone":

Litell Lowys my sone, I have perceived well by certeyne evidences thine abilite to lerne sciencez touchinge noumbres and proporciouns; and as wel considere I thy bisi preyere in special to lerne the Tretis of the Astrelabie. Than for as mechel as a philosofre seith, "He wrappeth him in his frend that condescendeth to the rihtful preiers of his frend," therfor have I geven the [thee] a suffisaunt [adequate] astralabie as for owre orizonte, compowned after the latitude of Oxenford, upon which by mediacion of this litel tretis I purpose to teche the [thee] a certain nombre of conclusions apertenyng to the same instrument. . . .

This tretis, divided in 5 parties, wole I shewe the [thee] under ful lihte rewles and naked wordes in Englissh, for Latyn ne kanstow [know you] yit but smal, my litel sone. But natheles, suffise to the [thee] thise trewe conclusiouns in Englissh, as wel as suffisith to thise noble clerkes Grekes thise same conclusiouns in Grek, and to Arabiens in Arabik, and to Jewes in Ebrew, and to the Latyn folk in Latyn; whiche Latyn folk han (had) hem [them] furst owt of othre diverse langages, and writen in hir [their] owne tonge, that is to sein, in Latyn. And God wot that in alle this langages, and in many mo, han thise conclusiouns ben suffisantly lerned and tawht, and yit by diverse rewles, ryht as diverse pathes leden diverse folk the ryhte wey to Roome. Now wol I prey mekely every discret persone that redith or herith this litel tretis, to have my rewde endytyng [composing] for excused, and my superfluite of wordes, for two causes. The firste cause is for [because] that curious enditing [complicated expression] and hard sentence [difficult meaning] is ful hevy [difficult] at ones for swich a child to lerne. And the seconde cause is this, that sothly me semeth [it seems to me] betre to writen unto a child twies a good sentence than he forgete it ones.[25]

Again we observe that the one time Chaucer does address a specific audience, it is not a wealthy patron but his son, the same sort of intimate circle as that implied by the dedication of *Troylus* to his friends Gower and Strode.

The introduction to the *Astrolabe* is Chaucer's most explicit statement about authorship. Other than this there are only the references of the persona to writing and reading within or at the end of so many of his poems. At the end of *Book of the Duchess* he will "be [in] processe of tyme,/ Fonde [try] to put this swevene [dream] in ryme" (1331–32); at the end of *Parliament of Fowls*, "I wok, and othere bokes tok me to, / To reede upon, and yit I rede alwey" (695–96); *House of Fame* breaks off incomplete but contains the allusion to his clerical work in the custom house and his reading at home cited above. The entreaty about his book at the end of *Troylus*, the command of Alceste that he write the legends of good women for the queen, and the address to posterity at the end of *Canterbury Tales* have been quoted above. Of these, only the reference in *House of Fame* to his work in the custom house is at all autobiographical. But the influential image of Chaucer as an author comes through in spite of his reticence—by his example, not by his assertion.

Realization of the presence of an author is one of Chaucer's contributions to the emergence of the individual in English literature. The other is his projection of the identities of the individual pilgrims and characters in the *Canterbury Tales* and *Troylus*. Although verisimilitude, or mimesis as it is called by Erich Auerbach,[26] was beginning to make its appearance in the French fabliaux and in the sophisticated presentations of character by Dante and Boccaccio, most literature to Chaucer's time was still highly conventional in its treatment of character. The medieval view of the community as *corpus Christi* envisaged society in terms of the functions of the estates, not in terms of individual initiative. Each estate had its prescribed tasks, and social criticism in the Middle Ages was complaint against the way in which individuals in the various estates failed to live up to their divinely assigned roles. This kind of social criticism began in the penitentials, which were handbooks to assist the confessor in the administration of penance.[27] These handbooks go back to the sixth century in Ireland, but the literature was greatly reinforced by the mandate of the Fourth Lateran Council (1215–1216) that every Christian must confess and be absolved at least once a year.

The most famous penitentials resulting from the Lateran Council were Raymond of Pennafort's *Summa de casibus* (Encyclopedia of sins, c. 1235) and Guilielmus Peraaldus's *Summa de vitiis et virtutibus* (Encyclopedia of vices and virtues, c. 1260). Versions of these handbooks spread throughout Europe. They were soon adapted for private moral instruction as in Frère Laurent Gallus's French *Le somme le roi* (The encyclopedia for the king, c. 1279) dedicated to the king of France. That served as the basis for William of Waddington's Anglo-Norman *Manuel des péchés* (c. 1300) and Robert Manning of Brunne's English adaptation *Handlyng Synne* (c. 1303; "handlying" is an interesting translation of *manuel*).

The shortcomings of the estates were treated in collections of *sermones ad status,* sermons addressed to particular estates, since medieval sins were class-based.[28] For example, pride and killing might be sins for a priest and not for a knight, while cowardice and poverty might be sins for a knight and not for a priest. But the satire on the estates was primarily a genre of Latin poetry beginning in the twelfth century,[29] like *Speculum stultorum* (Mirror of fools, 1180) by the Englishman Nigel Longchamps, the poems of Walter of Châtillon (d. 1202) and Walter Map (d. about 1208), and the goliardic poems criticizing the shortcomings of the clerical establishment. In the thirteenth century there are French estate poems like *Livre des maniéres* by Étienne de Fougères, chaplain to Henry II, and Rutebeuf's *L'État du monde* (c. 1265), and by the fourteenth century there are English treatments. Two treatments of this material in England but not in English are the long poems by Chaucer's friend John Gower, the French *Mirour de l'omme* and Latin *Vox Clamantis,* and the tradition underlies the social criticism in *Piers Plowman* and forms the basis for the long disquisition on the deadly sins in Chaucer's Parson's Tale.

Chaucer's contribution was to move perception of character away from the collective viewpoint of complaint about the failure of the estates to live up to their responsibilities to the specific viewpoint of modern satire, which evaluates behavior not in terms of a Divine Plan but in terms of individual human experience: what has come to be thought of as the "categorical imperative" of Immanuel Kant, that moral law is the product of human behavior, not human behavior the product of moral law.

This Copernican perception (as Kant called it) is what has made the General Prologue to the *Canterbury Tales* so basic in the evolution of English literature. Its definitive statement is by John M. Manly, *Some New Light on Chaucer* (1926), in which he identifies in Chaucer's London real-life models for the pilgrims. But this perception has been considerably altered by Jill Mann, *Chaucer and Medieval Estates Satire* (1973), which points out that Chaucer envisaged the pilgrims in the General Prologue very much in terms of the medieval estates.[30]

One innovation is that Chaucer begins his catalogue of pilgrims in the General Prologue with the highest secular estate: the Knight, his son the Squire, and his servant the Yeoman. Nearly all medieval treatments of the estates began with the pope and the religious and moved on to the king and the chivalry. Secularization of society is one of the most frequently remarked features of the evolution from medieval to the modern, and Chaucer was here marking himself as a modern. His second group is, however, the religious: the Prioress, the Monk, and the Friar. The third group is the professionals, who work with their minds, not with their hands: the Merchant, the Clerk, the Lawyer, and the Franklin. The fourth group is the skilled manual workers: the Artisans and their Cook, the Shipman, the Physician, and the Wife of Bath (who is a weaver as well as a wife). The lowest group on the social scale is the peasants: the Plowman and his brother the Parson. And the final group is the rascals: the Miller, the Manciple, the Reeve, the Summoner, and the Pardoner.

The competition proposed by the Host in the General Prologue marks the transition from the conception of the commune as a spiritually ordained organism to that of a voluntary assemblage. The Knight is the natural, God-ordained head of the pilgrim body in the Pauline sense of *corpus Christi*. But the Host says that he has a plan that will enliven the journey:

> "And if yow liketh alle [it pleases you all] by oon assent
> For to stonden at my juggement,
> And for to werken as I shal yow seye,
> To-morwe, whan ye riden by the weye,
> Now, by my fader soule that is deed,
> But ye be myrie, I wol yeve yow myn heed!
> Hoold up youre hondes, withouten moore speche."
>
> (CT 1.777–83)

And the assembled group consents:

> Us thoughte it was noght worth to make it wys,
> And graunted hym withouten moore avys.
>
> (CT 1.785–86)

The Host then proposes the story-telling competition, whose winner will be rewarded when they get back to the Tabard Inn with "a soper at oure aller cost" (1.799), and offers himself as their leader:

> "I wol myselven goodly with yow ryde,
> Right at myn owene cost, and be youre gyde,
> And whoso wole my juggement withseye
> Shal paye al that we spenden by the weye.
> And if ye vouchesauf that it be so,
> Tel me anon withouten wordes mo,
> And I wol erly shape me therfore."
>   This thyng was graunted, and oure othes swore
> With ful glad herte, and preyden hym also
> That he wolde vouchesauf for to do so,
> And that he wolde been oure governour.
>
> (CT 1.803–12)

The Host's campaign speech has been successful, and he is elected as their leader. Throughout the rest of the journey, the company enjoys the sort of political structure that England formalized after 1660. The Knight continues as the natural, hereditary leader, and when the Host requires correction or support, as at the end of the Pardoner's Tale and in the Nun's Priest's headlink, the Knight steps in. But the Host is the elected prime minister who superintends the details of the journey. What a nice parallel to the roles of the English queen and prime minister!

Chaucer does not present the estates mechanically. He groups the Parson in the peasant estate along with his sibling, the Plowman, instead of in the religious estate, perhaps as a commentary on the low repute into which the monastic orders had fallen after being for a thousand years the heart of Christendom. The Pardoner and the Summoner are likewise minions of the Church but grouped with the rascals, which provides commentary on the discredit of the system of indulgences and of the ecclesiastical courts. These two components of the medieval church were eliminated or reduced in the Counter-Reformation; it was the sale of pardons (indulgences) that led eventually to Martin Luther's break with Rome. The Knight, Parson, and Plowman are the only pilgrims presented without a trace of criticism, and they represent the traditional three estates: knight, priest, and peasant. The Lawyer's skill as a "purchasour" is a commentary on the breakdown of system of entailing estates that would finally bring about the demise of the feudal aristocracy. The Physician's appetite for money and collusion with the druggists are criticisms still voiced. And so on.

The qualities that make these figures universal is the iconic represen-tation, often by satiric inversion, of their ideal functions in the *corpus Christi*. Chaucer calls attention to these qualities before he begins their descriptions. His language is reminiscent of the instruction at the begin-ning of the penitential handbooks, that the priest should "diligently search out the circumstances both of the sinner and the sin, that from these he may prudently understand what manner of advice he ought to offer him and what sort of remedy he ought to apply."[31] As Chaucer phrases it:

> Me thynketh it acordaunt to resoun
> To telle yow al the condicioun

> Of ech of hem, so as it semed me,
> And whiche they weren, and of what degree,
> And eek in what array that they were inne.
>
> (*CT* 1.37–41)

The "condition" is the estate; "whiche" is the specific role in that estate (for example, in the estate of chivalry, knight, squire, baron, king); "in what degree" is the station in the hierarchy of the estate; "array" is the dress by which conditions and degrees were marked for all classes until the French Revolution, as they still are for the military.

What gives universality to the Knight is the underlying conception of "knighthood," to the Monk, the underlying conception of "monkhood," to the Wife of Bath, the underlying conception of "wifehood" (which was indeed one of the conditions in the traditional lists of estates). The detailed descriptions of the pilgrims are the bridge from the icon of the estate to the psychologically realized individual. In *Art and Illusion* (1960), E. H. Gombrich observes that "to the Middle Ages, the schema is the image; to the post-medieval artist, it is the beginning place for correcting adjustments, adaptations—the means to probe reality, to wrestle with the particular."[32] Most medieval depictions of people in art as well as in language are emblematic of their estates. In no case does the array of Chaucer's pilgrims contradict their estates, as it might in a modern novel or film, where a character in blue jeans could turn out to be the boss, and a character in business clothes the underling. The physiognomic treatises went further by finding connections between physical characteristics and moral dispositions, as the Franklin's sanguine complexion, and the Wife of Bath's gap teeth.[33]

Chaucer's achievement was to make the physical details at once representative of the schema and indicative of the particular. It is interesting how well the illustrator of the Ellesmere manuscript appreciated this dual significance. To insure that the observer would not miss the reference to the Monk's jingling bells, he hung them all over his horse, from ears to tail, and even on his hounds' collars. He bandaged the Cook's "mormal" like a major wound, and gilded the Miller's thumb and Physician's flask. Although the details are vividly personal, they clearly suggest the abstraction behind the image: the worldliness of the Monk, the vice of the Cook, the skill and avarice of the Miller and Physician.[34]

This mingling of emblematic and individual details has been admired by later writers, as we shall see in the last chapter. Roger Ascham in 1552 observed that "an historian" must be diligent to describe "the site of places and nature of persons not onely for the outward shape of the body: but also for the inward disposition of the mynde, as *Thucidides* doth in many places very trimly, and *Homer* everywhere. . . . And our *Chaucer* doth the same."[35] No doubt Shakespeare, Henry Fielding, Henry James, and Thomas Wolfe would have been able to achieve much the same effects without the example of Chaucer, but it is interesting to observe how clearly Chaucer's achievement has been recognized as literature has moved on toward psychological realism.

Chaucer went further than the physiognomists and typologists by pointing up the contradictory features of the pilgrims. The Knight displays all the chivalric virtues, but it is his antiheroic qualities that mark him as an individual: "of his port as meeke as is a mayde," "His hors weren goode, but he was nat gay," "Of fustian [coarse cloth] he wered a gypoun [tunic] / Al bismotered [soiled] with his habergeoun [chain mail]" (*CT* 1.69–76). These are not features of the archetype of the gorgeously appareled knight on a white horse, and they offer an interesting insight into what makes the difference between "heroism" and "chivalry" as we use the terms today. But most of all, they mark the Knight as an individual whom we would recognize if we met him at a parade.

The Prioress is a portrait of a good-hearted woman who nevertheless exemplifies the failings that led to the dissolution of the conventual system. We can smile at the airs she gives herself, her provincial French, and her concern for good manners, and we sympathize with her pity for dead mice, but we are brought up sharp when we are told she feeds her dogs "rosted flessh, or milk and wastel-breed" (*CT* 1.146). Few medieval peasants tasted meat once a year, much less refined "wastel," which is the Germanic form of French *gâteau*. Who was it who said "Let them eat cake"? Although the Prioress is not any more corrupt as a person than Marie Antoinette, her institution, like Marie's, caused so much hardship and misery in the real world that the only solution was to liquidate it, as aristocracy was liquidated after the French Revolution. Every item in the portrait of the Prioress implies criticism of her institution, but the details leave us sympathetic toward her unfulfilled femininity: her romance heroine's name Eglentyne; her devotion to the charismatic St. Loy (Elegius); her soft, red mouth; the ambiguous "Amor vincit omnia" on her rosary.

The Clerk's devotion to books and study, his unwillingness to "have office" (that is, accept a clerkship in a secular office), and his eagerness to impart his knowledge and principles are the archetype that give rise to the term "professor," one who professes, affirms, his subject. But the attitude of Chaucer the bureaucrat, who had to steal the hours for his own reading and writing from his six-day-a-week schedule in the custom office, must be as complicated as the attitude of present-day lawyers and doctors toward college professors. Lawyers and doctors, too, have to read and write and advise clients, but for forty or fifty hours a week, not just ten or twelve—and, of course, for many times what the academic earns.

Each of the pilgrims in the General Prologue emerges as a mimetic reality. But Roger Ascham put his finger on the principal way that the pilgrims are personalized. It was by exploring their intentions, the "inward disposition of the mynde." Their occupations, clothing, and horses are as much indications of their psyches as of their estates. This emphasis on intention is contrary to the Teutonic tradition. As Colin Morris points out in *The Discovery of the Individual, 1050–1200,*[36] both primitive Germanic customary law and early church regulations were indifferent to intention. The Teutonic penal codes prescribed punishments for actions, not for the intentions behind the actions. The same was true of the original penitentials, which attached penance for external acts rather than for internal states of mind. Concern for intention in the theological writings of the Mediterranean church fathers like Augustine and Jerome, and sensitivity to procedure and proof in Roman law engendered attention to motive in church law as it began to be canonized. This was further reinforced by the recovery of Aristotle's *Ethics* and by one of Abelard's most original works, *Ethics: or, Know Thyself* (1135), which defined sin solely by intention. Concern for inner righteousness was reinforced by the self-examination mandated by the promulgations of the Fourth Lateran Council and by the mystical and heretical movements of the later Middle Ages. In England, the Common Law, based on external actions and precedents, was an outgrowth of the Anglo-Saxon codes, but the Curia Regis, the King's Court, introduced by William the Conqueror, developed the law of equity, an outgrowth of canon law. The Curia Regis, presided over by the royal chaplain, the chancellor, "keeper of the king's conscience," made its decisions on the basis of fairness rather on the basis of precedent.

Attention to motive is one of the things that distinguishes romance from epic. Actions are the subject matter of the heroic poems like *Beowulf* and *Chanson de Roland,* but the inward dispositions of the lovers are the subject matter of the troubadour lyrics. The medieval romances combine the two motifs. Protagonists still perform heroic actions, but, like Tristan and Lancelot, they are frequently tormented by conflicting obligations. In Chrétien's *Lancelot,* the hero meditates on the shame before he clambers into the cart. In *Cligés,* Fenice meditates to herself several times about the difference between her affair with Cligés and Iseult's with Tristan: Iseult gave herself to both her husband and her lover while Fenice will preserve herself for her lover alone. C. S. Lewis in *The Allegory of Love* interprets the subject matter of the *Roman de la Rose* as the woman's internal debate over whether to accept or repulse her suitor, and the *dits* and *lais* of the French court poets are explorations of sentiment rather than narrations of plot.

Chaucer's early poems are concerned much more with inward disposition of the mind than with dramatic action. Like the French *dits,* they have no plots; nothing really "happens." In the *Book of the Duchess* the persona [?Chaucer] leads the Black Knight [?John of Gaunt] to talk as a way to assuage his sorrow over the death of his Fair White [?Blanche of Lancaster]. In *Parliament of Fowls* the contrast is between the futility of courtly love and the satisfactions of natural love, and between the sentimental posturings of the royal eagles and the sexual "need" of the common fowl. The point of *House of Fame* is less clear, but in it the poet/persona (called "Geffrey" by the eagle) seems to be wrestling with some personal problem: the nature of poetry? what sort of poetry he should write to achieve fame? his domestic situation with Philippa? It all depends on which critic you read. Not until he gets to *Troylus and Criseyde* and *Palamon and Arcite* (the Knight's Tale) does Chaucer venture upon a plot, and these two plots are, of course, derived from Boccaccio. There are sources or analogues for nearly every plot Chaucer develops in the Canterbury collection.[37] The same is true, of course, of Shakespeare and of Milton. The two Canterbury tales for which we do not have analogues are the Squire's Tale and the Tale of Sir Thopas, and in those the poet seems to be groping for direction. It almost appears that the fathers of English literature were incapable of creating original plots. But originality was not expected in literature until the advent of the novel—which is another story.

The plot of *Troylus* is merely the scaffolding for lyrical and philosophical meditation about emotions and intentions. It is an exploration of the motives of Criseyde, in particular, which is what led the early critics to call this poem the first English novel. Much of this psychological development was added by Chaucer. Criseyde's 230-line internal debate over whether to give up her liberty and succumb to love (2.701–931) is expanded from eighty lines in *Il Filostrato,* and the extensive exploration of the intentions of all three protagonists added to the poem after Pandarus thrusts the letter into Criseyde's bosom (2.1155) replaces four hundred lines of Baccocio with a thousand lines, nearly a fourth of the poem.

Chaucer's focus on intention reaches its high point in the confessions of the Wife of Bath, the Pardoner, and the Canon's Yeoman in the *Canterbury Tales*. Again, confessions as a literary device was not original with Chaucer.[38] The confessions of False-Semblant (Hypocrisy) and La Vielle (the old bawd) in *Roman de la Rose* are the immediate models for the Pardoner and the Wife of Bath. Confession as an aspect of the search for individuality (for Freud's *id*) was in the air, particularly in the testaments of mystics like St. Francis of Assisi and Meister Eckhart abroad and Richard Rolle and Margery Kempe at home. Abelard's *Historia Calamitatum* was perhaps the most dramatic. Dramatic monologues about inclinations and repugnances reveal character in the headlinks of the Miller, Man of Law, Merchant, and Franklin, and of the Host himself in the Monk's headlink.

Along with dramatic monologues of confession, the genre of debate provided insight into motive and intention.[39] Debates and colloquies were important medieval pedagogical techniques. On the elementary level, they provided audio-lingual practice in Latin, since all education until after the Renaissance was education in a foreign language. At a more advanced level, they provided practice in logic and persuasive argument, since all rhetoric was conceived as oral argument. These pedagogical colloquies found their way into poetic debates between the body and soul, the owl and the nightingale, the fox and the wolf, and so on. In *Canterbury Tales,* debates—quarrels—reveal the characters of the Miller and Reeve in their headlinks, of the Summoner and the Friar in the Wife of Bath's prologue and in their own headlinks and tales, and of the Host, Cook, and Manciple in the Manciple's prologue.

The treatment of the individual in Chaucer's poetry is the earliest representation in English of what David Reisman and his collaborators in *The Lonely Crowd* (1955) describe as the transition from tradition-directed culture to inner-directed culture.[40] In tradition-directed society the conformity of the individual is dictated by the power relations among various classes and clans which have endured for centuries and are modified only slightly, if at all, by successive generations. The culture controls every detail of individual behavior through economic compulsion, ritual, routine, and religion. In contrast, the inner-directed society is characterized by increased personal mobility. The greater choice this society provides and the greater initiative it requires in order to cope with the new problems call for character types often in conflict with traditional behavior. We can understand why the Wife of Bath emerged as Chaucer's most memorable character. But most of the pilgrims tell tales in tension with their prescribed roles. The Knight's Tale suggests the futility of noblesse oblige; the Man of Law's Tale raises questions about the dividends on the constancy of Constance; both the Wife of Bath's and Clerk's Tales refute the ideal of male supremacy; the Friar's Tale casts aspersions on ecclesiastical justice, and the Summoner's Tale on the medicant ideal. All of the miscreants in the fabliaux are in conflict with convention.

As the control of convention is called into question, a new psychological control appropriate to a more open society is required, which Riesman describes as a "psychological gyroscope." Once set in motion by parents and teachers, this gyroscope guides the inner-directed character no matter what the obstacles. Conflict between inner and outer direction is the stuff of both modern art and modern life, exemplified in the tensions of the "me" generation.

The conflict between convention and desire in *Gawain and the Green Knight* and between dogma and personal salvation in *Piers Plowman* show just as much sensitivity as Chaucer's to these tensions. But my phrasing of that sentence reveals the nature of Chaucer's contribution. *Gawain* is anonymous, and was not known before the nineteenth century; *Piers* is likewise anonymous, and was regarded as little more than a lollard tract until the middle of the present century. By hindsight, we can discern modern cultural tensions emerging in almost all literature as it approaches the Renaissance and Reformation, but the expression is more reflective than agential. The writing that influences change is the oeuvre of germinal thinkers like Abelard, Wyclif, and Luther. I believe that Chaucer ranks with Abelard and Wyclif as an agent of change, not merely as a mirror. The contribution of the germinal thinkers is primarily their ideas and secondarily the language in which the ideas are couched, although in Germany Luther's language (likewise a special adaptation of chancery language) was nearly as important as his ideas. The contribution of a poet is primarily the language he or she fashions to express the cardinal concerns of the society. "What oft was thought, but ne're so well express'd." We turn next to these verbal constructs in the poetry of Chaucer.

4.

The Chaucerian Voice

We must begin by again reminding ourselves of the difference between the position of Chaucer's writing during his lifetime and today. When Chaucer was writing, French was still the language of power and prestige; English was still a domestic patois. But it seems clear that English was becoming the colloquial for all classes, and that as it came to replace French for oral discourse in government and business it was developing into the Franglais, 50 percent Romance, that it is today. It was the function of Chaucer and a handful of other London writers between 1350 and 1400 (like John Gower and Thomas Usk, but not the provincial writers of the *Pearl* poems or *Piers Plowman*) to be the first to employ this bureaucratic Franglais for purposes of literature. For a variety of reasons, Chaucer's writings emerged as cynosures of this new literature. They were the most brilliant; they showed the greatest variety; they may have been actively sponsored by the king, as we shall see in the next chapter. Chaucer was the first to refer to the Franglais in the *Treatise on the Astrolabe* as the "King's English": "God save the King, that is lord of this langage."[1]

The Chaucerian voice has since the inception of literature in Modern English provided a touchstone for urbane, sophisticated expression. What are the elements of urbanity and sophistication? Integrity, courtesy, modesty, experience, intelligence, learning, wit, humor, irony, sympathy—we can make our own lists. But sophisticated English begins for most people with "Whan that Aprill with his shoures soote / The droghte of March hath perced to the roote."

It was probably important to the creation of the Chaucerian voice that Chaucer had no authoritative models of writing in English. We have no evidence that he had ever read any literary English. Scholars have pointed to the parody on minstrel style in the Tale of Sir Thopas and its references to other romances as evidence that he was familiar with English romances;[2] others have pointed to the homiletic style of the Parson's Tale as evidence that he knew English sermons;[3] still others have noted phrases and images that suggest that he knew English songs and lyrics.[4] This is all probably so, but it is all inference. He found no English model impressive enough to refer to. There is no indication that he knew the *Pearl* poems, or *Piers Plowman,* or the poems of his friend John Gower. When we compare this silence with the specific allusions to and borrowings from important authors and works in Latin, French, and Italian in nearly every one of his works, it becomes obvious that these were his real models. Chaucer's principal contribution was the fashioning of an English that could convey sophistication and learning as effectively as they were conveyed in these continental languages. For his audience, French and Latin were still the only possible literary languages. As we have observed before, fourteenth-century wills and library lists include few books in English, and the few cited are invariably ecclesiastical. The cultivated public waited to be shown that English was capable of sophisticated expression.

So Chaucer and his small circle created literary language nearly out of the whole cloth. The fact that Chaucer's English was so wholly colloquial may help to account for the "naturalness" of his poetic voice. It is amazing how much more natural his poetry is than his prose, particulary than his pioneering experiments in philosophical and scientific writing (*Boece, Melibee, Astrolabe,* and *Equatorie*). His technical prose is stiff and awkward. *Melibee* begins, "A yong man called Melibeus, mighty and riche, begat upon his wyf, that called was Prudence, a doghter which that called was Sophie." This translates almost exactly Chaucer's French original: "Uns jouvenceaulx appellez Mellibee, puis-sans et riches, ot une femme appellée Prudence, de laquelle il ot une fille." The eighteen words of French are more compact than the twenty-three words of English, and avoid the repetition of "that"; virtually all of Chaucer's prose suffers from this sort of verbosity, ambiguous reference, and awkward phrasing. Skeat and others have demonstrated at length how much more effective his Boethius is in his poetic renditions than in his prose translation.[5]

The amazing thing is that unlike this translation prose, Chaucer's verse, equally the product of translation, has the limpid, natural flow of conversation. The first two lines of *Canterbury Tales* call attention to themselves as literature by archaic grammar, French word order, and poetic inversion. "Whan that" instead of merely "Whan" preserves the Anglo-Saxon collocation of the adverb with relative "that" (found also in "which that" in the *Melibee* citation above); "shoures soote" achieves rhyme by using the French word order for the modifier; "droghte of March hath perced" achieves both rhythm and formality by putting the object before the verb. There are similar reversals in the following lines, but the idiom grows more and more spontaneous as it flows along. Keats said, "if poetry comes not [note his "literary" inversion!] as naturally as the leaves on a tree it had better not come at all."[6] What could be more natural than

> Whan Zephirus eek [also] with his sweete breeth
> Inspired hath [another metrical inversion] in every holt and
>   heeth
> The tendre croppes, and the yonge sonne
> Hath in the Ram his halfe cours yronne [another inversion],
> And smale foweles maken melodye,
> That slepen al the nyght with open eye—
> So priketh hem nature [another inversion] in hir corages—
> Thanne longen folk [another inversion] to goon on
>   pilgrimages,

And palmeres for to seken straunge strondes
To ferne halwes, kowthe [known] in sondry londes . . .

(*CT* 1.5–14)

The natural idioms are inlaid with words and inflections ("eek,"
"hath," "kowthe") that had become obsolete by the time of Wyatt and
Surrey, which reinforced the development of an artificial poetic diction
that poets have struggled against over the years, sometimes very specifically, like Wordswoth in *Lyrical Ballads* and T. S. Eliot in *The Wasteland*.
But Chaucer himself had no such tradition to contend with. Indeed, his
poetry is, like Shakespeare's, more colloquial than formal English will
now accept. It has less parallelism and subordination and often uses the
syntax of speech such as ellipsis ("And [we] made forward erly for to
ryse; And by his covenant [he] yaf rekenynge"), parataxis ("An horn he
bar, [whose] the bawdryk was of grene; Bad every wight [that] he
sholde go selle"), and anacoluthon, that is, grammatical shift within the
sentence ("The reule of seint Maure or seint Beneit, / By cause that it
was old and somdel streit [strict], / This ilke monk leet olde thynges
pace [pass]").

The naturalness of the idioms and speech rhythms are only the
foundation for the Chaucerian voice. The melody of the poetry bespeaks
a familiarity not only with the possibilities of oral performance but also
with the theoretical distinctions between the "artificial music" of song
and the "natural music" of recited verse that are distinguished by Eustache Deschamps in his *Art de dictier* (1392). The minstrel tradition was
still strong in the era before radio and television; songs and stories in
English must have been stock entertainment at every sort of public and
private gathering. There can be little doubt that Chaucer wrote many
of his poems with performance in mind—and modern actors find them
eminently performable.[7]

Oral recitation of narrative poetry had a long tradition, but the
lyric had originally been devised as song. Only in the fourteenth century
do we begin to find discussion of recitation rather than singing of

ballades, madrigals, rondeaux, and the other fixed forms codified by the French court poets. The regulations of the London Pui indicate that it was already hard to get members to sing their ballades. The Puis were religious, charitable, convivial civic organizations like modern Rotary Clubs.[8] They came into existence in southern France in the thirteenth century. Their purpose was to bring merchants and artisans together socially in periodic feasts. The original name, Confrérie de Notre Dame du Puy, suggests that the inspiration for the fraternity came from the celebrated, miracle-working statue of the Virgin in the cathedral of Le Puy en Velay in Auvergne, but before the end of the thirteenth century fraternities were found throughout France and the Low Countries and in London. The regulations of the London fraternity (written of course, in French), inserted in a 1320s letterbook of the London corporation, state that "the royal feast of the Pui is maintained and established principally for crowning a royal song." At each feast, the entertainment consisted of ballades composed and performed by the members, and a member was exempted from the twelve-pence dues at a meeting to which he came prepared with a new song. This mercantile assembly provides the most likely audience for the French ballades of Chaucer's friend John Gower, and would have been an ideal audience for some of Chaucer's own pieces. The regulations specify that

> although the becoming pleasance of virtuous ladies is a rightful theme and principal occasion for royal singing, and for composing and furnishing royal songs, nevertheless it is hereby provided that no lady or other woman ought to be at the great sitting of the Pui, for the reason that the members ought hereby to take example and rightful warning to honor, cherish, and commend all ladies, at all times, in all places, as much in their absence as in their presence.

One wonders whether these lofty sentiments were ever challenged by male chauvinist fabliaux like Chaucer's Merchant's or Shipman's Tales! But decorum aside, the regulations specify that two or three who understood singing were to be appointed to evaluate the music, "For without singing no one ought to call a composition of words [*une resoun endite*] a song, nor ought any royal song be crowned without the sweet sounds of melody sung." Evidently the brothers had some difficulty in encouraging singing rather than reciting. This is exactly the distinction that Deschamps made between artificial and natural music.

With the tradition of oral performance still strong, and the continued orality even of private reading, it is clear that the sound of the words lies behind the marvelous melody of the Chaucerian lines. "Whan that Aprill" displays the assonance of "a" through the first three words; "with his" the assonance of "i"; "shoures soote" the near alliteration of "sh/s" and near assonance of the "ou/oo." The next line returns to the "a" assonance for "March hath" and to the "o" for "to the roote" with subtle inversion of the vowel and "t."

Prosodists have devoted articles and books to the technique of Chaucer's verse,[9] but it is seldom remarked how few English models he had to learn from. That one of the earliest English poets should have been so gifted is an accident of genius that ranks alongside that of Shakespeare—but Shakespeare had the model of Chaucer, as well as Spenser, Marlow, and others for his prosody, no matter what we may think about the originality of his dramaturgy. I am not claiming that Chaucer invented assonance or alliteration, any more than that he invented metrical rhythm or the stanza forms he employs. Most of these are found in earlier and contemporary English verse and were common in the French and Italian poetry upon which he drew. My claim is that the brilliance of Chaucer's achievement and his prominence in society gave his poetry a special notoriety, and that his technique has provided a model for all ensuing poets in English.

To naturalness of expression and proficiency of technique Chaucer added substance. By the fourteenth century, love had become the obsessive subject for poetry, as evidenced by the regulations of the London Pui.[10] But, particularly in France (Italy was, as we shall see, different), it had become a fashion rather than a passion. The great age of the troubadours, of the French romances (like those of Chrétien de Troyes), and of creative allegory (like the *Roman de la Rose*) was past and French poetry had come to treat love as manners and polite behavior. This vulgarization had been implicit in the handbook on courtly love, *De arte honeste amandi* (c. 1190), by Andreas Capellanus, "chaplain to the king of France," which first set forth the relation between love and conduct." This relationship was codified in a series of model dialogues between men and women of the nobility, gentry, and middle class, displaying how the game of love—dalliance, flirtation—should be carried on within and between the classes. By the fourteenth century Andreas's literary fancy had become an etiquette that distinguished the gentle from the churl. In his chapter on the "The Court of Cupid" in *Poets and Princepleasers* (1980), Richard Firth Green has described how commonplace love poetry became. Every gentle (in the medieval sense) person was expected to sing love songs and write love poems. Such songs and poems had few artistic pretensions. They were simply, like clothes and manners, the marks of birth and breeding.

The love poems of Machaut, Deschamps, and Froissart are exemplifications of this court culture, distinguished more for technique than for substance. Their *dits* and *lais* continued to express the metaphoric identification of devotion to courtly ladies with personal discipline and feudal loyalty. These poems featured a minimum of narration and characterization, but were debates and complaints that explored the fine points of *courtoisie*—courtly behavior. Like the troubadour lyrics, these poems are usually first-person expressions of the personal sentiments of the poet-narrators. Saying came to take the place of doing. In the romances of Chrétien de Troyes, the mark of great heroes, like Lancelot or Tristan, was brave deeds and devoted service, not writing love poems—to do, not to say (although Tristan was indeed a great harper). By the fourteenth century, princes like Wenceslaus de Brabant and Charles d'Orléans in France had transformed the mark of courtly refinement from actual liaisons to the writing of ballades and rondeaux, as did Sir John Clanvowe (author of the *Boke of Cupide*) and James I of Scotland (probable author of the *Kingis Quair*) in England. Machaut's account of his affair with Toute Belle in *Livre dou voir dit,* discussed in the last chapter, is perhaps the supreme example of the sublimation of doing to telling.

Chaucer's earliest poem, *Book of the Duchess,* comes directly from this tradition. Like the French *dits,* it is composed of reverie and debate about courtly love, with a minimum of action. The poet-persona begins complaining that he has for eight years suffered from love sickness:

> But men myght axe me why soo
> I may not sleepe, and what me is.
> But natheles, who aske this
> Leseth his asking trewely.
> Myselven can not telle why
> The sothe; but trewly, as I gesse,
> I hold hit be a sicknesse
> That I have suffred this eight yeere—
> And yet my boote [cure] is never the nere [nearer],
> For there is phisicien but oon
> That may me hele.
>
> (*BD* 30–40)

He quickly turns from this introduction to recount the dream of his encounter with the Black Knight in the forest. The inspiration for this encounter is Machaut's *Jugement dou Roy de Behaigne,* but the transformation shows what I mean by Chaucer's "giving substance" to courtly cliché. In the *Jugement* the poet-narrator listens to a lady who has lost her lover through death argue with a knight who has lost his lover through betrayal about whether death or betrayal is the greater sorrow. This is a typical *question d'amour* of the sort that Andreas Capellanus had propounded for polite society to polish its intercourse. No actual death or betrayal is imagined; no real emotion is evoked. Chaucer, called upon to write an elegy on the death of Blanche, wife of his patron John of Gaunt, adapted the courtly dalliance of Machaut's poem to the real death of Blanche. The knight's stereotypical praise of his faithless lady in *Jugement* is transformed into the Black Knight's poignant lament for his dead lady. The language and details of the Black

Knight's description of his lady in *Duchess* are direct translations from Machaut, but the elegiac context provides an emotional charge lacking in the French. Both the context and narrative frame give meaning to the dialogue. Although the narrator knows the reason for the Black Knight's lament, he pretends not to know, and thus encourages the Knight to pour out his grief as consolation. Modern critics have found his technique nearly as skillful as that of a psycho-analyst.[12] So the vapid love talk of the *dits amoureux* is converted to psychotherapy, and a piece contrived almost wholly of lines translated from conventional poems by French court poets becomes serious.

The *Book of the Duchess* and the *Legend of Good Women* are the poems most reflective of the matter and language of French court poetry. Chaucer evidently returned to translation of the French *dits* in the *Legend* for the reasons I detailed in chapter 2. Discussion of Chaucer's direct indebtedness to the French was inaugurated by G. L. Kittredge and J. L. Lowes in a series of articles at the beginning of this century developing a suggestion made by Tyrwhitt in the eighteenth century that the prologue to the *Legend of Good Women* was based on the *marguerite* poems of Machaut, Froissart, and Deschamps.[13] These are a cluster of poems in honor of the *marguerite*, French for "daisy" as it is called in Chaucer's poem, employing the medieval symbolism of the daisy as the ideal of womanhood because of its purity (white) and humility (low to the ground), and because it follows the sun throughout the day and closes up at night when the sun is not present. Lowes went so far as to specify Deschamps's *Lay de franchise* as the source for lines 1–196 of Chaucer's prologue, and Froissart's *Paradis d'amoureus* as the source for lines 197 to the end, but current criticism tends to look more closely at Machaut's *Jugement dou Roy de Navarre*.[14]

This *dit* was written as a companion piece to Machaut's *Jugement dou Roy de Behaigne*, which treats the tragedies of the lovers, and *Navarre* purports to atone for the injustice toward women in that poem. The *Book of the Duchess* treats the tragedy of the Black Knight. Afterwards Chaucer wrote *Troylus and Criseyde*, and the prologue to the *Legend of*

Good Women purports to atone for the injustice toward women in *Troylus*. The king of Navarre assigns as punishment for the poet's heresy against women that he write a lay, a chanson, and a ballade. The king of love at the end of the prologue to the *Legend* assigns as punishment for the poet's heresy that the poet write the stories of love's martyrs. There are lines in the *Legend* prologue that could have been taken from any one of several of the French poems.

We can leave it to the scholars to debate the specific indebtednesses. Suffice it to say that, as with *Book of the Duchess,* nearly every line of the prologue to the *Legend* has a French source. The poet is again the lover, but this time defined from the beginning as an adulatory court admirer, not as an erotic suitor, and, as discussed in chapter 2, the prologue incorporates the sharpest criticism Chaucer ever made of the bad rule of Richard II. Recent critics have interpreted the Ovidian stories written to fulfill Alceste's command to make

> a glorious legende
> Of goode wymmen, maydenes and wyves,
> That weren trewe in lovyng al hire lyves;
> And telle of false men that hem bytraien
> (*LGW* 483–86)

as deliberate sabotage of the banal idealization of the cult of love.[15] The stories certainly depict love as agony rather than as felicity—which is the principal difference between the classical view of love as a destructive passion and the troubadour view of love as a civilizing sentiment. Whatever the occasion for the return to the courtly ideal in its prologue, the ultimate effect of the *Legend of Good Women* is the same sort of rejection of that ideal that we find at the end of the first book of *House of Fame,* when the dreamer finds himself in a wasteland after leaving the temple whose walls portray the lament of Dido over the falsity of Aeneas. In the next book of *Fame,* the eagle purports to bring the poet more reliable tidings of love, and in the last book the poet seems to conclude that he will never achieve fame writing about that subject.

In *Parliament of Fowls* the dreamer passes first through the surrealistic Temple of Love, filled with icons of sterility and unnatural passion, including some of the same names as the lovers in the *Legend*. He then goes out into a flowery glade where Dame Nature arranges for the birds to choose their mates in fertile, natural love. So Chaucer's early dream visions reject, each in its own way, the banality and sterility of the courtly cult, and substitute for it more genuine sentiments. All this is what I mean by Chaucer's "giving substance" to French conventions.

This deliberate rejection of the courtly stereotype is one of the things that has made Chaucer's art attractive since the advent of the novel, although it was the residue of courtly coloring that made his dream poems and *Troylus and Criseyde* more popular than *Canterbury Tales* until the time of Dryden. But it is the sheer variety of Chaucer's voices rather than the distinctiveness of any one voice that has provided a cynosure for subsequent writing in English. Let me try to distinguish between "voice" and "style." *Beowulf* and *Gawain and the Green Knight* have style but not voice. Style describes the external finish of the artifact: formal or informal, smooth or rough, simple or complicated. We speak of the "plain style," the "aureate style," the "didactic style." All of these describe the creation from the outside. *Beowulf* is written in epic style in that it is a serious narrative about a national hero. *Gawain* is is in romance (or shall we say romantic) style because the hero's erotic adventures are more important than his heroic. Chaucer himself writes in an intimate style because he so often intrudes upon his narrative line. But in each case, style focuses on the finished artifact, not upon the intentions of the author, the process of his composition, or the reception by the audience. Style is the topic of formalist rather than of psychological criticism.

Awareness of the relationship between author and audience as codified in the *ars dictaminis* was commonplace in the Middle Ages, as I argued in chapter 2. It provided the idea for the multiple voices of the *Canterbury Tales*. But the psycho- and sociolinguistic awareness that we have come, since about 1950, to designate as "voice" was largely lacking in earlier discussions of style. The conception of voice incorporates both elements of the rhetorical dialectic. It is the voice that every speaker/ author assumes in the light of, on the one hand, his purpose in speaking and, on the other, his conception of the receptivity of his audience. It is the voice that any persona or character assumes in any imaginary situation. The situation may range from one as personal as a husband speaking to a wife to one as impersonal as an author writing a page; from scrawling a letter to a lover to composing an official report. I oversimplify by categorizing all voices under three general headings: narrative, lyric, and rhetorical.

The narrative voice is that which takes least account of intention and reception. It is the voice I designated above as style. The style can be either narrative or dramatic; in the terminology of Wayne Booth in *The Rhetoric of Fiction,*[16] it can be either "telling" or "showing." But in either case, the substance of such communication is the message/story itself, not the psychology of creation and reception. If narrative, it is usually in the third person, omniscient, and rendered with a minimum of editorial interference. This is the voice of *Beowulf* and *Gawain.* All aspects of action and motivation are described; little inference is called for on the part of the audience. We may, of course, infer about the intention and reception from the style employed and the actions described, as much modern criticism is now undertaking to do, but the method is what Booth describes as telling rather than showing. But showing can be nearly as impersonal as telling. This is the dramatic form of narrative, in which the actors and actions convey the message directly. Their own voices must, or course, be lyric or rhetorical, and more inference is called for on the part of the audience. But the overall voice of *Hamlet* or *Macbeth,* in which author does not obtrude and there is no overt address to the audience, is much the same as that of the impersonal narrative.

The impersonal narrative voice has been and continues to be the most common in expository writing, fiction, and drama. But an important feature of the Renaissance was the reemergence of the voice of the author. This voice, which I designate as lyric, is the "I" discussed at some length in the last chapter. But even though Chaucer's voice emerges as one of the most distinctive in English, it is not this personal voice. We have several times remarked upon Chaucer's silence about his own sentiments and experiences. He has very few pieces that are in any way personal. Of his eighteen short poems, five are narrative or dramatic. The *Complaint unto Pity* and *Balade of Pity* are in the first person but clearly conventional. They are abortive experiments in expressing courtly conventions in English, as the "Ch" poems discussed in the first chapter express them in French. The lovely ballades *Womanly Noblesse* and *To Rosemounde,* in the same adulatory voice as the prologue to *Legend of Good Women,* must have been intended as compliments to great ladies of the court. It appears that Chaucer was not comfortable with this lyric voice and quickly moved to transform it in *Book of the Duchess* and the ensuing dream poems.

His "Boethian ballades," *Truth, Gentilesse, Lak of Steadfastnesse,* and perhaps *The Former Age,* appear to express concern about the corruption of the court of Richard II; *Bukton, Scogan,* and *Adam Scryven* are to friends, probably the most personal poems he ever wrote; and *Fortune* and *Complaint to His Purse* are entreaties to Richard and then Henry for money. But these are all in what I designate the rhetorical voice.

The Chaucerian voice is essentially what I define as rhetorical. Its predominant characteristic is its self-conscious engagement with the writing process and with the reactions of an audience, and its awareness of the comparable strategies of classical and continental authors. This level of sophistication began to emerge with the revival of classical education in the twelfth century, as discussed above. As the vernaculars began to explore richer subject matter, they, too, began to employ the rhetorical voice. Richard Firth Green describes the progressive displacement of the minstrel entertainer by the sophisticated court poet in the thirteenth and fourteenth centuries.[17] The court poet thought of himself as moralist, historian, educator, counselor, and propagandist. Most of Chaucer's contemporaries and successors—the *Gawain* poet, Langland,

Gower, Hoccleve, Lydgate—saw themselves in these roles. Chaucer's ironic self-depreciation prevented him from lecturing the king and the magnates directly, the way Gower does, and, for whatever reason, he eschewed any direct comments on historical events, but he clearly thought of himself as educator and moralist. It has been suggested that his translations of Boethius, *Melibee,* and the Parson's Tale were made at the command of Richard II's mother, Joan of Kent, to assist with the young king's education.[18] Attractive as it is, this idea is fraught with difficulties, since it assumes that Richard's education would have been in English, which, as discussed in chapter 1, is highly unlikely. Nevertheless, Chaucer was, as Deschamps's ballade discussed in chapter 2 gives evidence, recognized as a great translator and philosopher, educating his countrymen in courtly decorum and morality.

One of Chaucer's favorite rhetorical questions is whether the stories in *Canterbury Tales* contribute to "sentence" or "solas," that is, to instruction or pleasure. In the Parson's Tale there is a line deprecating giving rewards "for veyne glorie, as to mynstrals" (*CT* 10.813), and it is interesting that in Fame's great hall the dreamer first meets the "mynstralles / And gestiours that tellen tales" (*HF* 1197–98) before seeing that the roof of the hall is supported by the great poets of antiquity, like Homer, Virgil, Ovid, Lucan. And as he is contemplating these famous poets

> ther come entryng into the halle
> A ryght gret companye withalle,
> And that of sondry regiouns,
> Of alleskynnes condiciouns
> That duelle in erthe under the mone,
> Pore and ryche.
>
> (*HF* 1527–32)

Chaucer may not have yet planned the varied company that would immortalize his *Canterbury Tales,* but it must be more than serendipity that led him to describe in the General Prologue

Wel nyne and twenty in a compaignye
Of sondry folk, by adventure yfalle
In felaweship, and pilgrimes were they alle.
(*CT* 1.24–25)

The rhetorical voice is the voice of the "serious" Latin literature that so influenced Chaucer's development, especially Boethius in his dialogue with Lady Philosophy, but also Horace, Juvenal, Seneca, and other Latin writers that Chaucer had studied in school. Most influential of all must have been Ovid, whose specific influence we will discuss at the end of this chapter. This rhetorical voice was imitated by the medieval scholastic poets like Alanus ab Insulis, whose expression of the contrast between sterile unnatural love and fertile natural love in *De Planctu Naturae* (The Plaint of nature) is acknowledged in *Parliament of Fowls*, and John of Salisbury, Walter Map, and others whom Chaucer may or may not have known.

But Chaucer had a more immediate model than Latin for his rhetorical voice. This was Jean de Meun's continuation of the *Roman de la Rose*. Guillaume de Lorris's evocation of the court of love in the first part of the *Roman* (c. 1237) provided an epitomy of the idea of love as a civilizing agency that helped to establish courtly love as the principle theme in medieval poetry. The voice of the dreamer being educated by his pursuit of the rose became the voice for Dante in *Vita Nuova*, Petrarch in his *Canzonieri*, Machaut and the French court poets, and Chaucer at the beginning of *Book of the Duchess* and *Legend of Good Women*. But the romantic voice of Guillaume was offset in the latter two thirds of the *Roman de la Rose* by the rhetorical voice of Jean de Meun (c. 1277), who used the narrative thread for rationalistic, philosophical, satiric discourses on love, sex, theology, learning, politics, and almost everything else under the sun. Chaucer's literary career may be described as a progress from the romantic voice of Guillaume to the rhetorical voice of Jean de Meun.[19] Dante and the Italian poets followed Jean de Meun in giving substance to the courtly conventions. The lyrics in *Vita*

Nuova express vapid troubadour sentiments, but the prose frame in which they are embedded provides structure for the mystical spiritualization of love in *Divine Comedy*. Boccaccio gave psychological verisimilitude to artificial courtly situations in *Teseide* and *Philostrato,* upon which Chaucer based the Knight's Tale and *Troylus and Criseyde.* Who can say how or why Chaucer came to reject the conventional lyric voice in favor of the rational rhetorical voice, but this is the essence of the achievement that he bequeathed to subsequent writers in English.

Some aspects of the rhetorical voice derive directly from medieval rhetorical theory. The most important feature of Ciceronian rhetoric for the Italians who created *ars dictaminis* was the *exordium,* the opening, which was intended to render the audience attentive and well disposed. The art of dictation was, after all, the art of writing persuasive letters. All else depended upon capturing the good will of the reader. This concern can be explained both by the subservient position of the scribes in the illiterate power structure and the diplomatic nature of their compositions. At any rate, the greatest attention in the medieval manuals of *dictamen* described by James Murphy in *Rhetoric in the Middle Ages* was on techniques by which to capture the sympathy of the audience.[20] Proverbs and other aphoristic wisdom were advocated as especially useful in establishing concord. Collections of sententia that were *dictamen*-centered were compiled, some of them multilingual, and proverb examples were included in the discussions of *captatio benevolentiae* (capturing good will) in the manuals. Chaucer's affinity for proverbs, catalogued long ago by B. J. Whiting in *Chaucer's Use of Proverbs* and by many critics since,[21] may be seen in this light as a considered device by which to identify himself with his audience, as well as yet another indication of the influence of the *ars dictaminis* on the creation of his style.

Another aspect of the rhetorical voice particularly related to the *ars dictaminis* is the awareness of writing as a process rather than as a product. The dictaminal manuals are first and foremost textbooks on the process of composition. To take an almost random example, the *Summa de constructione* begins (c. 1252, Murphy's translation):

Because it is necessary for dictatores to know how to compose Latin writings both coherently and ornately—and in this consists the whole dictaminal science—and since ornament was fully treated in my book on dictamen beginning "De competenti dogmate," I, Master Pons of Provence, who wrote the book just named for the benefit of my young students, now transmit a slight though complete book concerning construction. Know therefore that construction in grammar is said to be in three modes.[22]

This is the sort of textbook that young Geoffrey must have used in the inns of chancery, and from it learned to view himself as a professional writer, not as the troubadour entertaining his patrons.

Chaucer was not unique, of course, in viewing writing as a process. In the previous chapter we noted that many of Petrarch's letters deal with the intentions and processes of his compositions; Machaut's *Livre dou voir dit* (1364) turns from his love affair to his process of composition and the arrangement of his oeuvre; and Deschamps's *L'art de dictier et de fere chançons, balades, virelais, et rondeaux* (1392) was the the first vernacular treatise on the process of literary composition. This self-consciousness about writing as a process, and inference about the conditions under which it would be received, that originated in the epistolary situation of the *ars dictaminis* led eventually to the very personal voices of Montaigne, Bacon, Sir Thomas Brown, and other Renaissance writers whose essays sound so much like Petrarch's letters to the world. So Chaucer was merely reflecting the sophisticated literary sensitivity of his time when he wrote with triple vision—with one eye on his story, another on his audience, and the third on his own process of composing.

At the beginning of *Book of the Duchess* the narrator's voice is more lyric than rhetorical, but at the beginning of *Parliament of Fowls* we can hear the voice shifting deliberately from lyric to rhetoric:

> The lyf so short, the craft so long to lerne,
> Th'assay so hard, so sharp the conquerynge,
> The dredful [frightening] joy alwey that slit so yerne
> [slips away so quickly]—

> Al this mene I be Love that my felynge
> Astonyeth with his wondyrful werkynge.
>
> (*PF* 1–5)

Continuity with the lyric voice is preserved in these opening lines by applying the aphorism "ars longa, vita brevis" to the art of love instead of the art of poetry. But the voice soon shifts from the participatory to the critical as the narrator goes on:

> Yit happeth me ful ofte in bokes rede
> Of his [Love's] myrakles and crewel yre.
>
> (*PF* 10–11).

From there on the *Parliament* is devoted to exploring a variety of loves and voices.

The *House of Fame* has been interpreted as dealing directly with Chaucer's concern about the purpose and subject matter of his writing.[23] After viewing the love tragedy of Dido, the dreamer-narrator finds himself in a wasteland. A golden eagle from Dante's *Divine Comedy* swoops down ostensibly to carry him from the erotic wasteland of *amor* up into the world of Dante's spiritual *agape*. But the eagle turns out to be a pedantic schoolmaster concerned with teaching him only the physical facts about poetry and the universe when what the narrator wants is poetic inspiration. When the eagle proposes to teach him astronomy, he demurs:

> "No fors," quod y, "hyt is no nede.
> I leve [believe] as wel, so God me spede,
> Hem that write of this matere [the stars],
> As though I knew her [their] places here;
> And eke they shynen here so bryght,
> Hyt shulde shenden [destroy] al my syght
> To loke on hem."
>
> (*HF* 1011–17)

In the hall of Fame, he sees the great poets of antiquity and appears to look forward to the Canterbury pilgrims as his own great subject.

None of this yet deals directly with the process of composition. Chaucer emerges as a self-conscious process poet in *Troylus and Criseyde*. He is not there a participant in the action, as he becomes in *Canterbury Tales*, but from the first lines, the poem is as much about the narrator's intentions and the reaction of the audience as about the story of the lovers.

> The double sorwe of Troylus to tellen,
> That was the Kyng Priamus sone of Troye,
> In lovynge, how his aventures fellen
> Fro wo to wele [good fortune], and after out of joye,
> My purpos is, er that I parte fro ye.
> Thesiphone, thow help me for t'endite
> These woful vers, that wepen as I write.
>
> (*TC* 1.1–7)

Thesiphone who is here invoked is one of the Greek Furies. All three sides of the semantic triangle are specified: the sender, "My purpose"; the receivers, "parte fro ye"; and the message, "the double sorwe of Troylus." The next two stanzas begin with authorial "I." The fourth through the seventh stanzas are addressed to "ye loveres, that bathen in gladnesse." In the seventh, the "I" makes covenant with the "you" to have empathy with all lovers (1.47–51) before turning to the story.

The authorial voice in *Troylus* has been praised as a model of how the author of written literature can achieve empathy with and shape the response of the inferred audience. Frequently it simply tells them how they ought to react:

> Forthi [therefore] ensample [example] taketh of this man,
> Ye wyse, proude, and worthi folkes alle,
> To scornen Love, which that so soone kan
> The fredom of youre hertes to hym thralle [enslave];
> For evere it was, and evere it shal bifalle
> That Love is he that alle thing may bynde,
> For may no man fordo [avoid] the lawe of kynde [nature].
>
> (*TC* 1.232–38)

The good will of the reader/audience is conjured through the compliment "ye wyse and worthi folkes"; the concluding aphorism is right out of the *dictamen* tradition. And author and audience unite in wonder at the mystery of love's power.

Modern literary criticism takes its departure from the notion of the reciprocity of the communication process, from the belief that a message is composed as much from what the imagination of the receiver supplies as from the details the sender provides. Dieter Mehl has pointed out with what genius Chaucer employed this technique in *Troylus and Criseyde*.[24] For example, at the end of Book 2, Troylus lies in his feigned illness waiting for Pandarus and Criseyde to enter the room:

> But now to yow, ye loveres that ben here,
> Was Troylus nought in a kankedort [stew, a nonce word],
> That lay and myghte whysprynge of hem here,
> And thought, "O Lord, ryght now renneth my sort [fortune]
> Fully to dye or han anoon confort!"
> And was the firste tyme he shulde hire preye
> Of [for] love: O myghti God, what shal he seye?
>
> (*TC* 2.1751–57)

At which point Book 2 ends. Book 3 begins with forty-nine lines of proem; then it picks up the story:

> Lay al this menewhile Troylus
> Recordyng his lesson in this manere.
>
> (*TC* 3.50–51)

"Al this menewhile" obviously refers to the time it has taken for the reader to get through the proem. Mehl compares this to Sterne in *Tristram Shandy:* "It is about an hour and a half's tolerable good reading since my Uncle Toby rung the bell."[25]

Readers must fill in gaps in the information and make inferences and judgments about the nature of the action. The central ambiguity in Chaucer's poem is the character of Criseyde: her apparent reluctance in the case of Troylus and her easy compliance in the case of Diomede. After she has been aroused in the wonderful Freudian scene where Troylus rides by on his way from battle, "For bothe he hadde a body and a myght / To don that thing . . ." (2.633–34)—the double entendre of "that thing" being very evident—the narrator comes to her defense:

> Now myghte som envious jangle thus,
> "This was a sodeyn love. How myght it be
> That she so lightly loved Troylus,
> Right for the firste syghte, ye, parde?"
> Now whoso seith so, mot [may] he nevere the [prosper]!
> For everythyng a gynnyng hath it nede
> Er al be wrought, withouten ony drede [doubt].
>
> For I sey nought that she so sodeynly
> Yaf hym hire love, but that she gan enclyne
> To lyke hym first, and I have told yow why.
> And after that, his manhod and his pyne [pain]
> Made love withinne hire herte for to myne [mine, burrow],
> For which by proces and by good servise
> He gat hire love, and in no sodeyn wyse.
>
> (*TC* 2.666–79)

But when she accepts Diomede, the narrator shares the reader's distress:

> But trewely, how longe it was bytwene
> That she forsok hym for this Diomede
> Ther is noon auctour telleth it, I wene.
> Tak every man now to his bokes hede:
> He shal no terme [explanations] fynden, out of drede
>   [doubt].
> For though that he [Diomede] gan for to wowe hire sone
>   [soon, immediately],
> Er he hire wan yet was ther more to done.
> Ne me ne lyst [desire] this sely [foolish] womman chyde
> Ferther than this story wol devyse.

> Hire name, allas, is punysshed so wyde
> That for hire gilt it oughte ynow [enough] suffise.
> And yf I myghte excuse hire ony wyse,
> For she so sory was for hire untrouthe,
> Iwys, I wolde excuse hire yet for routhe [pity].
>
> (*TC* 5.1086–99)

Mehl cites a similar deliberate obfuscation of chronology at the end of *Mansfield Park,* where Jane Austen writes, "I purposely abstain from dates on this occasion, that every one may be at liberty to fix their own, aware that the cure of unconquerable passions and the transfer of unchanging attachments must vary much as to time in different people."[26]

Again and again, the reader is called on to fill in and to make moral and psychological judgments. When Criseyde promises Troylus that she will return to Troy within ten days, although it is manifest that she will not, the narrator editorializes:

> And trewelyche, as wreten wel I fynde,
> That al this thyng was seyd of good entente,
> And that hire herte trewe was and kynde
> Towardes hym, and spak right as she mente,
> And that she starf [died] for wo neigh whan she wente,
> And was in purpos evere to be trewe:
> Thus writen they that of hire werkes knewe.
>
> (*TC* 4.1415–21)

This process of inferring and evaluating is the rhetorical voice par excellence. Fielding, Sterne, and Austen may not have learned it from Chaucer, but its masterful employment is one of the reasons for the continuing importance of Chaucer's poetry in English literature.

The rhetoric of *Canterbury Tales* advances beyond that of *Troylus*. One of the liveliest critical debates is about whether the pilgrim "I" who narrates the frame and two tales of the Canterbury collection is Chaucer himself or is a persona with different perceptions from Chaucer's.[27]

There is a very real question as to whether literary sophistication by Chaucer's time had developed to the point where an author could create a narrator whose perceptions were different from his own, as Swift did with Lemuel Gulliver, Robert Browning with the three narrators of *Ring and the Book,* Ring Lardner in "Haircut," and Henry James with many of his narrators. This is what Wayne Booth designates as the "unreliable narrator" whose point of view becomes the essence of the story.[28] No one has argued that the "I" in *Divine Comedy, Roman de la Rose,* or *Livre dou voir dit* does not speak for the author, is not a reliable narrator. Boccaccio in the pseudoautobiographical settings for his stories raises more of a question, and when presumed clerics purvey immoralities, like Andreas Capellanus in *De arte honeste amandi* or the Archpriest of Hita in *Libro de buen amor,* the voices may indeed be ironic. But whatever the degrees of sophistication of narrative voices as European literature approached the Rennaissance, there can be no doubt that the ambiguous voices and points of view in the *Canterbury Tales* introduced a new dimension into English literature.

Chaucer began experimenting very early with ambiguity in characterization and expression. In one of the first critical interpretations, G. L. Kittredge discussed the "naive" narrator of *Book of the Duchess* who could not understand that the Black Knight's lady was dead, and whose "obtuse" questions gave the knight the excuse to talk. Only in 1952 did Bertrand Bronson suggest that the narrator was deliberately prompting the Black Knight to therapeutic recall.[29] The dramatic if hardly equivocal voices of the birds in *Parliament of Fowls* and the exquisitely ambiguous voices of Criseyde and Pandarus appear to be rehearsals for the technique immortalized in *Canterbury Tales.*

It is impossible to be dogmatic about the reliability of Chaucer the author and unreliablility of Chaucer the pilgrim in *Canterbury Tales.* When the narrator says of the reprehensible self-characterization by the Monk in the General Prologue "And I seyde his opinioun was good" (*CT* I.183), he is either very naive or very ironic. When he depicts himself as distracted and "elvyssh" in Part 7, and goes on to tell first the uncouth tale of Sir Thopas and then the supermoralistic exemplum of Melibee, he becomes as complicated a personality as the Pardoner or the Wife of Bath. Richard Firth Green observes that the two tales told by the persona, a minstrel entertainment and a political sermon, exemplify the evolution of the poet in medieval court culture from entertainer to counselor. Yet most of the narrator's editorial comments, as when he advises the readers that if they do not like the bawdry of the Miller they should "Turne over the leef and chese another tale" (*CT* 1.3177), are rhetorical. As in *Troylus and Criseyde,* these comments draw the audience into the creative process, asking it to cooperate in making inferences, decisions, and evaluations.

The rhetorical voice asking the audience to cooperate in evaluating the ambiguities of the narrative introduces yet another element into English literature, that is, irony.[30] In making such a statement I must distinguish between irony in literature and irony in life. The fabric of existence is compounded of irony. In the broadest sense, irony is merely a recognition of contrast. If acknowledged directly, the recognition is realism, which Chaucer was also instrumental in introducing into English literature; if acknowledged obliquely, the recognition is irony. Structural and dramatic irony depend largely on the attitude of the observer, and there is much debate as to the degree of irony in the structure of Homer's epics, the Bible, Dante's *Divine Comedy,* or Shakespeare's plays. Juxtapositions that may be straightforward to one observer may be ironic to another. Verbal irony is calling attention to the contrast by inverse expression, as by calling bad good and sad happy. In the Old Testament, Job means just the opposite when he replies to the mindless optimism of his friends, "No doubt but ye are the people, and wisdom shall die with you" (12:2). Like structural irony, verbal irony can go unperceived by the unwary, as in *Oedipus the King* and *Tale of a Tub.*

Structural and dramatic irony have existed in all art and literature as they do in Chaucer, but they were not recognized, at least in English, until the seventeenth century (the first *OED* citation of this meaning for irony is 1649). But verbal irony was recognized as a figure of speech by Cicero's definition of Socrates' speech as *eironia*, from the Greek term meaning deliberate dissimulation, and by St. Augustine when he observed, "In irony we indicate by tone of voice the meaning we wish to convey, as when we say to a man who is behaving badly, 'You are doing well.' "[31] In medieval rhetorics, irony was a recognized figure of speech associated with allegory, a derisive mode of saying the opposite of what is meant. As with Cicero and Augustine, it depended on tone of voice. Presumably Chaucer read his poetry aloud, and it would save countless pages of print if we had a tape of his intonation as he recited the narrator's comment on the Monk cited above, "And I seyde his opinioun was good," or the Host's reaction to the Franklin's fulsome praise of the "gentility" of the Squire's awkward tale, "Straw for youre gentilesse!" (*CT* 5.695). Irony is even more ambiguous in writing than it is in speaking.

The irony of the Chaucerian voice is principally what modern critics designate irony of manner: self-deprecatory, smoothing over every roughness with understatement and humor. This manner, appropriate to the role of the courtier and diplomat, contributes to capturing the good will of the audience—enjoined by the *ars dictaminis*. But it could lead a critic like Matthew Arnold to deny that Chaucer is one of the great classics because he lacked "high seriousness." For example (the illustration is mine, not Arnold's), after Arcite's death in the Knight's Tale has been described in as purple a passage as Chaucer ever achieved (*CT* 1.2765–2807), the narrator goes on:

His laste word was, "Mercy, Emelye!"
His spirit chaunged hous and wente ther
As I cam nevere, I kan nat tellen wher.
Therfore I stynte [stop], I nam no divinistre [theologian];
Of soules fynde I nat in this registre,
Ne me ne list thilke opinions to telle
Of hem, though that they writen wher they dwelle.
Arcite is coold, ther Mars his soule gye [guide].

> Now wol I speken forth of Emelye.
> Shrighte [shrieked] Emelye, and howleth Palamon . . .
>
> (*CT* 1.2808–17]

Chaucer's introduction of an ironic narrative voice is matched by his introduction of a satiric view of character and behavior. Again, satire was a highly developed form in classical literature, but for a variety of reasons outlined by John Peter in *Complaint and Satire in Early English Literature,* what we today call satire all but disappeared as a literary genre from the fifth to the fifteenth centuries.[32] During this millenium, the criticism of society that medieval rhetoricians called satire was didactic rather than satiric. It focused on how individuals and classes fell short of the Platonic ideals envisaged for them, not on the incongruity of their actual behavior. This kind of criticism was exemplified in the penitentials and Latin estates poems discussed in chapter 3. The treatment of the vices and virtues in this complaint tradition is conceptual and allegorical whereas satire focuses on the concrete peculiarities of the individual. Complaint literature was essentially hortatory, intended to improve the behavior of the recipients. Chaucer's satire, like that of Swift and of E. B. White, betrays no desire for reform but is intended simply to delight. It is addressed to a reader not himself being subjected to criticism, who can therefore sit back and appreciate the satirist's shrewd hits on the faults of others. The voice of complaint literature is monotonous and impersonal, striving, like the Christianity it espouses, always to be sober and reasonable. The delight of Chaucer's voices is their variety and individuality—their urbanity, irony, malevolence, raillery, scurrility, cynicism.[33]

The difference between the voices of satire and of complaint can be observed in the individuality of Chaucer's voices compared with the generality of the voices of his contemporaries, John Gower, William Langland, and the *Gawain* poet. These are none of them mean poets, but none of the voices in their poems have provided such touchstones of verbal art as the voices of the *Troylus* narrator, Chaucer the pilgrim, the Wife of Bath, or the Pardoner.

All of the late fourteenth-century literary voices share the democratizing tendency that I associate with Chaucer's training in the inns of court. The view of man in courtly literature was essentially heroic—Beowulf, Roland, Tristan, Lancelot. Literature produced for the feudal aristocracy exemplified the values of that society. But as John Burrow says in *Ricardian Poetry*,[34] in Chaucer's culture man was no longer regarded as heroic but as humorous and ironic. There are no "heroes" in Chaucer, any more than in Gower or Langland; and the whole point of *Gawain and the Green Knight* is to show the moral flaw in one of the heroes of the Arthurian court. The very conception of a hero is monolithic: One can be the "best" knight or saint, or second or third best, but one cannot be "different." The penitential and mystical ethos of the later Middle Ages began to discount this sort of monolithy and exalt variety. David Riesman and his coauthors in *The Lonely Crowd* contrast the ideal of diversity in modern culture with the ideal of uniformity in medieval culture.[35] All of the Ricardian authors are in one way or another critical of medieval totalitarianism, but Chaucer's criticism is the most accepting of human diversity.

Chaucer grows increasingly critical as time goes by. The *Book of the Duchess* is hardly at all critical; criticism begins to appear in *House of Fame* and *Parliament of Fowls*. I will leave aside *Troylus* and *Legend of Good Women*, although some critics find them more than a little satirical. But the human comedy of *Canterbury Tales* marks a milestone in the evolution of satiric criticism that was not equalled until Ben Jonson and Jonathan Swift. Chaucer's critical voice may have been representative of the drift of perception in his period, but his language and technique were the most influential in conveying the significance of the new world view.

One of the most sophisticated aspects of Chaucer's technique is its power to juxtapose and shift. This is the principal attraction of the plan of *Canterbury Tales*, whose structure allows us to contrast religious and secular points of view, moralistic and bawdy, aristocratic and democratic, idealistic and satiric, and so on.[36] But the contrasts in points of view go beyond merely the personalities of the pilgrims and their tales. The point of view can shift from line to line. For example, the description of the Friar in the General Prologue begins from the narrator's viewpoint:

> A frere ther was, a wantowne [wanton, morally lax] and a
>   merye . . .
> He was an esy man to yeve penaunce
> Ther as he wiste to have a good pitaunce.

But in the next line he goes on:

> For unto a poure ordre for to yive
> Is signe that a man is wel yshryve,
> For if he yaf, he dorste make avaunt,
> He wiste that a man was repentaunt.
>
> (*CT* 1.207, 223–28)

Without transition but perfectly coherently, the point of view has shifted from that of the narrator to that of the Friar himself, providing an ironic commentary on the hypocrisy of the Friar and the corruption of compounding penance for money payment, which is what brought the indulgence system into such disrepute. John Crow Ransom used to say, "The wonderful thing about Chaucer is that you can never tell who's getting the bird."[37] The kaleidoscope of viewpoints makes every line in the General Prologue, and indeed in all of Chaucer's poetry, a new adventure each time it is read.

And so to the final and perhaps the most important quality of the Chaucerian voice, its humanism. Nothing distinguishes the medieval world view from the modern more than its distrust of the visible cosmos. Nearly all of the other differences, in human relations, in economics, in science, derive from the medieval elevation of spirituality over materialism. John Henry Newman in the opening chapter of *Apologia Pro Vita Sua* remarks several times that from the time he was a child, the world of the imagination was more real to him than the physical world around him.[38] This must have been the sensibility of most of Europe from the fall of Rome to the Renaissance, whenever and wherever that rebirth may be supposed to have occurred. The intellectual element of the reawakening has been called "humanism," which means concern for the human rather than the spiritual dimension of the universe. I have already noted this concern in connection with the emergence of the sense of individual in Chaucer's poetry. I may go on now to say that the conviction of the value of all things human and temporal that permeates Chaucer's writing is one of the qualities that makes his writing, along with that of Shakespeare, the foundation of modern literature in English—and, of course, as the earlier, his work occupies a special place. Spenser, Donne, and Milton are the last great exponents in English literature affirming the allegorical view of the universe. In the eighteenth and nineteenth centuries they rivaled Chaucer and Shakespeare in popular esteem, but in the twentieth they have begun to fade.

Preoccupation with the temporal world does not mean that Chaucer was an agnostic. His most important works, *Troylus and Criseyde* and *Canterbury Tales,* end with sincere and, in the case of *Troylus,* exquisite testimonials to his orthodox faith. The Boethian ballades, the Man of Law's Tale, the prologue to the Second Nun's Tale, the Parson's Tale, *ABC,* and other pieces breathe confident acquiescence to traditional Christianity. Some critics have seen him growing more preoccupied with religion as he grows older. But the essential difference is that Chaucer never perceived life as a dream, as an allegory, as the unsubstantial manifestation of a Platonic reality. Nothing could be farther from Chaucer's humanism than Newman's description of his own feeling of separation from tangible reality: "I thought life might be a dream, or I an Angel, and all this world a deception, my fellow-angels by a playful device concealing themselves from me, and deceiving me with the semblance of a material world." [39]

This sense of isolation from reality was manifested in the characteristic literary genres of the Middle Ages, dream vision and allegory. The two were combined in the most influential poem of the period, *Roman de la Rose*. Later French poets tended to reject the allegorical application of the dream vision, but they applied the form to exemplary indoctrination in courtly behavior, nearly as unreal to the majority of society as the allegory of love. Chaucer's first three poems are experiments in French dream indoctrination, with the variations we have already noted. But in his two great poems, he broke with the dream tradition to tell stories of real people living in the real world. Boccaccio and other Italians had made the same break; so this may be an aspect of the Italian influence on his work. Dramatic verisimilitude of the sort that Chaucer found in Boccaccio—and in Dante, even though *Divine Comedy* is still couched in a dream—is the eventual mark of the novel as compared with the romance. Chaucer never, except in the prologue to *Legend of Good Women* and the short poem "A Complaint unto Pity," used personifications or allegory. His pilgrims and the characters in the stories they tell may represent universal types or qualities, but they always act and speak, like Macbeth and Hamlet, as self-motivating human beings.

The sense of actuality produced by Chaucer's writing is a product of consummate artistry. It is never historical truth, but always the illusion of reality. Chaucer was the archetypical impressionist. We have mentioned repeatedly his silences, his incompletenesses, his shifts in style and point of view. Critics have cited his impressionistic employment of northern dialect markers in the Reeve's Tale.[40] The melding of bawdry and scholastic learning in the prologue to the Wife of Bath's Tale is one of the wonders of artistic creation. How can this pastiche of passages taken directly from antifeminist anthologies have produced the "realist" character in the *Canterbury Tales*—the only character referred to by other pilgrims (the Clerk and the Merchant, *CT* 4.1170 and 1685), and by Chaucer himself outside the Canterbury collection (in the ballade to his friend Bukton)?

The Canterbury pilgrimage ranks with the imaginary travels of Swift's Gulliver and Bunyan's Christian as one of the great journeys in English literature, yet in comparison with those we have virtually no information about the details. We know where it begins but not where it ends. There are five references to towns along the pilgrims' way, but the preferred order for the tales puts Rochester, forty miles from London, after Sittingbourne, only thirty miles from London. Scholars ever since Furnivall and Jusserand have tried to correct and fill in the details that Chaucer omitted, but that misses the point. These details would be of little interest if Chaucer's account had not already created the sense of actuality. Producing that sense, securing the "willing suspension of disbelief," had been the objective of classical literature as it is of modern literature. The only realism in medieval literature was in the chivalric romance, but that reality was limited to the world of the feudal aristocracy. As humanism and democracy began to emerge after the twelfth century, we begin to see realism in the fabliaux. But overshadowing these limited perceptions of reality was the universal perception of allegorical unreality that lasted until the enlightenment.

Humanism as generally understood means reawakened awareness of the concern for the real world as realized in classical literature. It is no accident that Chaucer was the first English author to turn to the Latin classics for models and illustrations. This is nowhere more evident than in his treatment of love. As Denis de Rougemont detailed in his mad but fascinating *Love in the Western World*,[41] a principal difference between the classical and medieval world views is their treatments of love. In the Latin classics, passionate love like that of Paris and Helen, Aeneas and Dido, or Antony and Cleopatra is a disease that destroys personal and communal stability. In medieval literature after the twelfth century, romantic love like that of Lancelot and Guinevere or Tristan and Isolt became an inspiration for heroism and civility. Chaucer began in *Book of the Duchess* with the inspirational conception, but from there on, we see him turning more and more toward the classical view of love as a figure for the irrational impulses of the human mind.

Troylus and Criseyde is an especially interesting exploration of the two conceptions. On the one hand, Troylus appears to exemplify the inspirational ideal. After Pandarus has promised to help him secure Criseyde at the end of Book 1,

> Troylus lay tho no lengere down,
> But up anoon upon his stede bay,
> And in the feld he pleyde the lyoun.
> Wo was that Grek that with hym mette that day!
> And yn the town his manere tho forth ay
> So goodly was, and gat hym so yn grace,
> That eche hym loved that loked on his face.
>
> (*TC* 1.1072–77)

And so on through another stanza. At the end of Book 3 (lines 1771–1807), the refining effects of love are again extolled. The most moving expression of the courtly ideal is Criseyde's words at the end of Book 4, just before she goes off to the Greek camp:

> "For trusteth wel that youre estat royal,
> Ne veyn [vain, sensual] delit, nor oonly worthinesse
> Of yow in werre or torney marcial [marshall],
> Ne pompe, array, nobley, or ek richesse
> Ne made me to rewe [have pity] on youre destresse.
> But moral vertu, grounded upon trouthe,
> That was the cause I first hadde on yow routhe [pity].
>
> "Ek gentil herte and manhod that ye hadde;
> And that yet hadde, as me thoughte, in despit
> Everythyng that souned into [inclined toward] badde,
> As rudenesse and pepelyssh [vulgar] appetit;
> And that yowre reson brydled youre delit—
> This made aboven every creature
> That I was youre, and shal while I may dure."
>
> (*TC* 4.1667–80)

But the irony is that Criseyde delivers this noble speech just as she goes off to perjure with Diomede. Troylus's behavior becomes faintly, or to some critics more than faintly, ridiculous as the poem progresses, and Criseyde's behavior exemplifies the irrationality of human emotions.

Ovid was the great master in using the comic irony of love to explore the incongruities of personality and behavior. It is no accident that the stories in *Legend of Good Women,* which have been called the training ground for the technique of the short stories in *Canterbury Tales,* are all adaptations from Ovid.[42] By the time Chaucer reaches *Canterbury Tales,* the treatment of love has become almost completely an index to incongruity rather than a pattern for perfection. In *House of Fame,* the eagle refers "Geffrey" to his "oune boke," Ovid's *Metamorphoses* (*HF* 712). John Fyler in *Chaucer and Ovid*[43] finds Ovid the model for nearly all aspects of the Chaucerian voice. He provides a model not only for the self-conscious, obtrusive author-narrator, but for untrustworthy narrators who in the letters of the *Heroides* provide rationalizations for deceptions and betrayals. Ovid's *Metamorphoses* epitomize the instability of forms and conceptions. Chaucer reveals a similar skepticism as he questions the forms of knowledge. He never questions orthodox Christianity directly, and he makes frequent acknowledgment of Divine authority, as at the end of *Troylus* and *Canterbury Tales.* But it is interesting how again and again his narrators and characters question the essential verities.[44] This is particularly true in his two most serious poems, *Troylus* and the Knight's Tale, into both of which he introduces agnostic comments not found in Boccaccio. Palamon, lamenting his fate after Arcite has been released from prison, complains:

> "O crueel goddes that governe
> This world with byndyng of youre word eterne,
> And writen in the table of atthamaunt [adamant],
> Youre parlement and youre eterne graunt,
> What is mankynde moore unto you holde
> Than is the sheep that rouketh [cowers] in the folde?
> For slayn is man right as another beest,
> And dwelleth eek in prison and arreest,
> And hath siknesse and greet adversitee,
> And ofte tymes gilteless, pardee.
> > "What governance [theory of government] is in this
> > prescience [providence],

That giltelees tormenteth innocence?
And yet encresseth this al my penaunce,
That man is bounden to his observaunce [duty],
For Goddes sake, to letten [refrain] of his wille [desire],
Ther as [whereas] a beest may al his lust [desire] fulfille.
And whan a beest is deed he hath no peyne,
But after his deeth man moot wepe and pleyne [complain],
Though in this world he have care and wo.
Withouten doute it may stonden [stand] so.
The answere of this lete I to dyvynys [divines,theologians],
But wel I woot that in this world greet pyne ys."

(CT 1.1303–24)

This is the sentiment of a dramatic character, but it expresses the same questioning of the universe as the narrator's reaction to Arcite's death, quoted above, and the marvelous conclusion to *Troylus and Criseyde:*

Swych fyn [such an end] hath, lo, this Troylus for love;
Swych fyn hath al his grete worthynesse;
Swich fyn hath his estat real [royal] above;
Swich fyn his lust [pleasure, passion], swich fyn hath his
      noblesse;
Swych fyn hath false worldes brotelnesse [brittlenesse,
      instability]!
And thus bigan his lovyng of Criseyde,
As I have told, and yn this wyse he deyde.

O yonge, fresshe folkes, he or she,
In which that love up groweth with youre age,
Repeyreth hom fro [from] worldly vanyte,
And of youre herte up casteth the visage
To thilke [that] God that after his ymage
Yow made; and thynketh al nys but a fayre [fair,
      circus]
This world that passeth soone as floures fayre.

(TC 5.1828–41)

The despairing conclusion is followed by the devout admonition that has so puzzled the critics, but the skepticism is just as characteristic of the Chaucerian voice as is the Christian optimism. Ovid's skepticism tends to be more epistemological and Chaucer's more devout, but the questioning voice is the same. What distinguishes the narrators of Ovid and Chaucer from those of Virgil and Dante, says Fyler, is that they are self-consciously trapped in the limitations of humanity.[45] The effect is comic irony, but irony that celebrates the nobility while it points up the fragility of the human condition.

The ironic voice, the humanistic world view, awareness of the individual, awareness of the audience, awareness of a world outside the court and the church, a sense of the power of the English language to express "the best that has been thought and said"—these are the qualities that account for the importance of Chaucer. To what extent have these qualities been recognized over the years, and how influential have they been in molding subsequent literature? To these questions we turn in the last chapter.

5.

Chaucer since 1400

It would appear that until 1400, writing in English was regarded largely as a curiosity. This may help to explain why we have no Chaucer manuscripts (except possibly the holograph of the *Equatorie of the Planets*) that date from before his death in 1400. Scholars find it hard to believe that such manuscripts did not at one time exist. The way that literature was preserved and disseminated until after the advent of printing was by circulating manuscripts from hand to hand and copying, or having copied, the pieces that appealed to one's personal tastes.[1] After 1350 this process became more formal, with the growing demand for business writing and for books, and the consequent development of a profession of public stenographers (called scriveners or stationers—the guild of scriveners is first mentioned in London in 1357), who wrote from dictation or copied upon commission at a penny or so per page.[2] But all writing continued to be "bespoke," that is, individually ordered and paid for, until after the advent of printing. Caxton in the epilogue to the first book printed in English, *Recuyell of the Historyes of Troye* (1476), explained that he found that he had promised copies of his translation to so many people that he had to take recourse to the new technology of printing "to thende that every man might have them attones [at once]."[3] So it is evident that printing was not the cause but the result of increased literacy, and that, as Marshall McLuhan observed, printing was the first step towards technological mass production—the creation of products on speculation to be stockpiled for sale upon demand, a process only now emerging in third-world economies.[4]

That Chaucer's poems were not disseminated throughout London during his lifetime in written form seems impossible to believe, but that all traces of such copies would disappear is equally hard to believe. The fact is, however, that the case of Chaucer is not exceptional. There are very few manuscripts of any secular literature in English dating from before 1400.[5] The famous Auchinleck and other manuscripts containing romances are not exceptions, since they occur in collections of religious literature. Manuscripts containing works of the other fourteenth-century writers in English like John Mandeville (or its English translation), John Trevisa, Laurence Minot, and John Barbour all date from after 1400—some from very long after. Nearly all manuscripts in English before 1400 were ecclesiastical—missionary works written by educated clergy for the edification of the uneducated laity. Sometimes these penitential and homiletic collections incorporated delightful surprises like "The Owl and the Nightingale" and the Middle English love lyrics, but only by accident and in unique manuscripts, clearly never intended for circulation. And in Chaucer's time, the dissenting pamphlets and poems of the lollards had brought even ecclesiastical English writing into disrepute.[6]

The survival of some twenty-six of the sixty-two manuscripts of John Gower's English frame poem *Confessio Amantis* dating from before Gower's death in 1408 is an exception. Why did Gower's pre-1408 manuscripts survive if Chaucer's did not? Because of Gower's own initiative. All of these manuscripts appear to have been commissioned by Gower himself.[7] They are handsomely drawn up and extremely correct, written to be presented to influential individuals like Thomas, Duke of Gloucester, or Henry Bolingbroke himself. Once a manuscript passed into such responsible hands as these, its chances for survival were pretty good. The history of the Gower manuscripts is to this extent—perhaps unflatteringly—different from the history of the Chaucer manuscripts, most of which are rather plain, commercial productions. The history of the *Piers Plowman* manuscripts is very much like that of the Chaucer manuscripts. Of the fifty-two extant, only four date from the fourteenth century.[8] The *Pearl* and *Gawain and the Green Knight* survive only in the amateurish manuscript Cotton A.x dating from about 1400.

Clearly the fine Gower manuscripts are exceptions. There was no demand in England before 1400 for copies of secular writings in English; "literature" still implied writings in Latin or French, as witnessed by all fourteenth-century library lists and the many fine manuscripts of Latin and French classics. Chaucer himself obviously saw no advantage in commissioning manuscripts for presentation—why, we do not know. Furthermore, as suggested in the first chapter, there was little in Chaucer's domestic situation or in his racy fabliaux to augur immortality. The one associate who clearly did read his works was no great help. Thomas Usk, whose apologia for his own unfortunate life, *Testament of Love*, designated Chaucer "the noble philosophical poete in Englissh," and quoted from *Boece, House of Fame, Legend of Good Women*, and *Troylus*, was a questionable character who changed sides several times in the political struggles between the king and the the appellant lords and was finally executed for treason in 1388. Admiration from a source such as this would merely confirm the disrepute of writing in English.

It has been customary to imagine that Chaucer was a popular entertainer in the royal courts and inns of court, but if so it was in oral performance rather than through written manuscripts. Over the years many people may have heard him read, but it seems likely that when Chaucer died in 1400, he left on his desk bundles of uncirculated and uncopied manuscripts, some like *Book of the Duchess, Parliament of Fowls, Troylus*, and *Boece* fairly complete, others like *House of Fame, Legend of Good Women, Canterbury Tales, Treatise on the Astrolabe*, and *Equatorie of the Planets* still in process of composition.[9]

The years immediately following Chaucer's death in 1400 saw the dawn of a new linguistic era. In 1399, Henry IV's claim to the throne and Chief Justice Thirnyng's address deposing Richard II are recorded in English in the Rolls of Parliament, and from then on there are an increasing number of English entries in the Rolls. Argument in Parliament had been conducted in English for nearly a century, but actions had continued to be recorded in the Latin and French of the Norman ascendancy. Beginning with Henry IV, what E. F. Jacob called the "pauper government" of the Lancastrians required popular acceptance of its usurpation and taxes and provisions for its warfare.[10] Recording the actions of government in English was a step towards securing parliamentary and municipal support, and the English signet letters of Henry V eventually provided a vestige of authority for linguistic nationalism.[11]

But authority in government was not necessarily cultural authority. If the Lancastrian administration was in any way consciously seeking popular support by strengthening the use of the vernacular, it needed socially accepted models of English. In about 1393, before Henry Bolingbroke became king, Gower changed the dedication of *Confessio Amantis* from Richard to Henry, and after he assumed the throne Henry must have encouraged Gower to compose *In Praise of Peace* defending his usurpation.[12] His son Henry eventually employed English for his signet letters. In the period from 1399 to 1417, the royal establishment appears to have undertaken a program to elevate the prestige of English. This took the form of encouraging the production of a body of sophisticated writing in the national language. Personal commentary—letters, diaries—was still so scarce in England that we have no record of such intention, but the circumstantial evidence is strong. The public relations agent for the program appears to have been the poet John Lydgate and the writer chosen to exemplify the new culture, Geoffrey Chaucer.

During the first decade of the century, the most influential counselors to the king and the prince were their close relatives the Beauforts—John, Earl of Somerset, who died in 1410; Henry, Bishop of Lincoln and Winchester, who became Lord Chancellor in 1403; and Thomas, who became Duke of Exeter in 1416. These three were half-brothers to Henry IV, sons of John of Gaunt by Katherine Swynford, while Henry was the son of John of Gaunt by Blanche of Lancaster (about whose death Chaucer had written his first poem). Philippa Chaucer was the sister of Katherine Swynford, which made Phillipa's son Thomas Chaucer at least first cousin to the Beauforts—half-brother to both the Beauforts and the king if Gaunt was Thomas's father, as discussed in chapter 1. As bastards, legitimated only after 1397, and regarded as upstarts by the regular aristocracy, the Beauforts were eager supporters of any move that would consolidate Lancastrian authority over the Anglo-Norman ascendancy.[13]

Thomas Chaucer's seat, after he married the heiress Maud Bergersh in about 1395, was at Ewelme, where he is buried. Ewelme is about ten miles from Oxford where in 1398 Henry Beaufort was chancellor of the University. Henry Beaufort is described in the chronicles as Prince Henry's tutor, and from about 1398–1403 Prince Henry, age eleven to sixteen, may have been in residence at Oxford from time to time under Henry Beaufort's tutelage.[14] From about 1397 John Lydgate may likewise have been in residence at Oxford. In 1408 Prince Henry wrote (in French) to the abbot of Bury St. Edmunds, the monastery of which Lydgate was nominally a member throughout his long and busy career, asking him to give Lydgate permission to continue his studies at Oxford.[15]

The lack of personal commentary makes it impossible to recreate any linguistic politics of the Prince Henry-Henry Beaufort-Thomas Chaucer-John Lydgate group except to observe how closely the individuals concerned were intertwined both in the records and by literary allusions. Thomas Chaucer was a relative and the recipient of many preferments from both Henry IV and V. As Speaker of the House of Commons periodically from 1407 onwards, he was involved in the process of communication between the government and the people. Promoting the national language for such communication appears to have been one of the Lancastrian strategies. Developing a recognized canon of literature in English could have been another. At any rate, it seems that soon after Chaucer's death, Thomas may have been encouraged to sift through his father's foul papers and commission production of authoritative versions of his most important works. The eight earliest manuscripts of *Canterbury Tales* appear to be systematic experiments designed to achieve the best presentation of the materials and to culminate in the sumptuous Ellesmere manuscript (c. 1410) with its pictures of the pilgrims and equestrian portrait of Chaucer.[16] There is no evidence who commissioned these early manuscripts, but the Ellesmere has been by Manly and Rickert tentatively traced back to Thomas Chaucer, who had the financial means, the best access to the prototypes, and the greatest motive for the editing.[17] Someone also commissioned the handsome Morgan Library manuscript of *Troylus and Criseyde* whose first page is decorated with the coat of arms of Prince Henry before he became king in 1413. And the Fairfax manuscript (c. 1430) that preserves most of Chaucer's minor poems contains poems ascribed to William de la Pole, Duke of Suffolk and husband to Thomas's daughter Alice.[18] Prince Henry along with his friend Edmund Lacy, master of University College until 1400 when he became king's clerk, is credited by John Norton-Smith with encouraging Lydgate to write poems in aureate English.[19]

That Chaucer was selected as more of a cynosure for the national language than Gower is a tribute both to the quality of his writings and his connection with the royal family. We have no documentary evidence that Prince Henry officially sponsored the use of English and designated Chaucer as the cynosure, but in 1412 he commissioned Lydgate to produce an English version of the Troy story in support of his ideal of military heroism. Its dedication comes as close as anything we have to attributing a language policy to Prince Henry. The prince, says Lydgate,

> comaunded the drery pitus fate
> Of hem of Troye in englysche to translate . . .
> By-cause he wolde to hyge and lowe
> The noble story openly wer knowe
> In oure tonge, aboute in every age,
> And y-writen as wel in oure langage
> As in latyn or in frensche it is;
> That of the story the trouthe we may nat mys

No more than doth eche other nacioun:
This was the fyn [end] of his entencioun.
                    (*Troy Book* 105–06, 111–18)[20]

And, says Lydgate, Chaucer provided the model for the language:

The hool story Chaucer kan yow telle
Yif that ye liste, no man bet alyve,
Nor the processe halfe so well discryve
        [describe],
For he owre englische gilt [gilded] with his sawes
        [sayings],
Rude and boistous [crude] firste be olde dawes
        [days],
That [it] was ful fer from al perfeccioun,
And but of litel reputaticoun,
Til that he cam & thorug his poetrie
Gan oure tonge firste to magnifie,
And adourne it with his elloquence.
To whom honour laude & reverence
Thorugh-oute this londe yove [given] & be songe
So that the laurer [laurel] of oure englische
        tonge
Be to hym yove for his excellence.
                    (*Troy Book* 3.4234–47)

Lydgate's *Life of our Lady* is likewise ascribed to the "excitation and stirryng of our worshipfull prince, kyng Harry the fifthe,"[21] and in at least three other poems before 1410 and in half a dozen afterwards he pays tribute to his "master Chaucer" from whom he learned his art. Recent critics have richly confirmed this Chaucerian influence.

In 1411 or 1412 Thomas Hoccleve, a clerk in the king's privy seal office, likewise dedicated his *Regement of Princes* to his "hye and noble prince" Henry. It opens with a dialogue between Hoccleve and a beggar who says (ironically, since Hoccleve's work in the office must have been in Latin and French):

> Al-thogh thou seye that thou in latyn,
> Ne in frenssh nowther [neither], canst but smal
> endite [compose],
> In englyssh tonge canst thou wel afyn [polish].
>
> *(Regement* 1870–72)[22]

Then Hoccleve goes on to acknowledge the influence of Chaucer:

> Mi dere maistir—god his soule quyte [reward]!—
> And fadir, Chaucer, fayn wolde han [willingly
> would have] me taght;
> But I was dul, and lerned lite or naght.
>
> *(Regement* 2077–79)

Beside still a third acknowledgment in three manuscripts of the *Regement* stands the famous portrait of Chaucer, which is thought to be the exemplar for the Ellesmere and other contemporary portraits.[23]

In a 1407 ballade addressed to Prince Henry and his brothers, Henry Scogan likewise praises his "mayster Chaucer / That in his langage was so curious," and quotes Chaucer's "Moral Balade of Gentilesse" as part of his poem.[24] In *Five Hundred Years of Chaucer Criticism and Allusion, 1357–1900,* Caroline Spurgeon quotes a 1410 tribute by John Walton, Canon of Osenay, to the "rhethoryk / In englisshe tong" of both Chaucer and Gower, and many other acknowledgments in the fifteenth century.[25]

Perhaps the most significant acknowledgment of Chaucer's priority is Caxton's preface to his second edition of *Canterbury Tales* (1484). It is noteworthy that Caxton printed nothing earlier than Chaucer and Gower. For him, English began with these two. His brief prologue to Gower's *Confessio Amantis* makes no comment on its precedence, but the prologue to the *Canterbury Tales* sounds nearly like an official pronouncement:

> Grete thankes, lawde and honour ought to be gyven unto the clerkes,
> poetes and historiographs that have wreton many noble bokes of wyse-

dom, of the lyves, passions and myracles of holy sayntes, of hystoryes of noble and famous actes and faittes, and of the cronycles sith the begynnyng of the creacion of the world unto thys present tyme, by whyche we ben dayly enformed and have knowleche of many thynges of whom we shold not have knowen, yf they had not left to us theyr monumentis wreton. Emong whom and in especial tofore alle other we ought to gyve a syngular laude unto that noble and grete philosopher, Geffrey Chaucer, the whiche for his ornate wrytyng in our tongue maye wel have the name of a laureate poete. For tofore that he by hys labour enbelysshyd, ornated and made faire our Englisshe, in thys royaume was had rude speche and incongrue, as yet it appiereth by olde bookes whyche at thys day ought not to have place ne be compared emong ne to hys bueauteuous volumes and aournate writynes. Of whom he made many bokes and treatyces of many a noble historye as wel in metre as in ryme and prose; and them so craftyly made that he comprehended hys maters in short, quyck and hye sentences, eschewyng prolyxyte, castyng away the chaf of superfluyte, and shewyng the pyked grayn of sentence utteryd by crafty and sugred eloquence.[26]

The allusions reveal that the admiration for Chaucer and, secondarily, Gower as innovators of literary language continued as long as there was distrust about the capacity of English. After his death, Lydgate himself was joined to Chaucer and Gower, and this triumvirate became a cliché of the origin of the national language—the Homer, Virgil, and Petrarch of English—cited in many allusions in Spurgeon until the seventeenth century. The most famous allusion to the first two is in Sir Philip Sidney's *Apologie for Poetrie* (1581) that has been called the first important English essay in literary criticism:

> So in the Italian language, the first that made it aspire to be a Treasure-house of Science, were the Poets *Dante, Boccace,* and *Petrarch.* So in our English were *Gower* and *Chawcer.* After Whom, encouraged and delighted with theyr excellent fore-going, others have followed, to beautifie our mother tongue, as wel in the same kinde as in other Arts.[27]

The last allusion linking all three that I find in Spurgeon is by John Bodenham in 1600.

Chaucer remained a model for writers of English until the language had changed so much that he could not be readily understood. This stage was ushered in on the one hand by the archaizing tendencies of Spenser, which encouraged the development of a poetic diction distinct from common speech that continues still, even though resisted by Robert Burns, Wordsworth, T. S. Eliot, or the American rap poets. Spenser more than any of his contemporaries appreciated and sought to emulate the music of Chaucer's verse. But Spenser's contemporaries, like Ben Jonson in *Timber* (c. 1630), recognized the artificiality of his language and his archaism as a model:

> And as it is fit to reade the best Authors to youth first so let them be of the openest and clearest: As *Livy* before *Salust*, *Sydney* before *Donne*: and beware of letting them taste *Gower* or *Chaucer* at first, lest falling too much in love with Antiquity, and not apprehending the weight, they grow rough and barren in language only. . . . *Spencer*, in affecting the Ancients writ no Language: Yet I would have him read for his matter; but as *Virgil* read *Ennius*.[28]

And Thomas Speght in his editions of 1598 and 1602 shifted Chaucer's role from that of a model for emulation in the use of English to that of a classic whose language and subject matter had to be glossed and annotated, just like that of any classic Latin or Greek author.

The tendency to regard Chaucer as a contemporary, which lingered on until after Tyrwhitt's edition in 1775, led to the deprecation of his "rough" meter and "archaic" vocabulary. These "defects" were countered in two ways. The first was by modernizing his spelling and regularizing his meter according to modern pronunciation. This process had begun in the earliest manuscripts and editions. It reached its zenith in the edition of John Urry (1721) that has been called "the worst text of Chaucer ever produced."[29] It is, indeed, the least faithful to the Middle English original, but compensation for loss of syllabic final *e*, *en*, and *ed* by addition of syllables and words ("idone" for "done," "began" for "gan," "which that" for "which," and so on) was a deliberate and systematic effort to adapt his verse to eighteenth-century pronunciation. The same thing was done for Shakespeare and Milton, of course, and it is interesting that whereas new-spelling Chaucers have always been regarded as heresy, new-spelling Shakespeares and Miltons have continued to be regarded as essential. The difference is that the sound of Shakespeare and Milton is less affected by modernization than the sound of Chaucer.

The second way in which Chaucer's archaism was countered was by "modernizing" his text. This began with Dryden's translations of the Knight's Tale, the Nun's Priest's Tale, the Wife of Bath's Tale, and the Character of a Good Parson from the General Prologue in his *Fables Ancient and Modern* (1700). These translations gained for Chaucer more popular attention than he had ever received, as attested by the enormous increase in the number of allusions in Spurgeon (86 entries from 1680–1699, 188 entries 1700–1720), and inaugurated a tradition of translation that has continued ever since—from Pope and John Gay, to Wordsworth and Leigh Hunt, to Coghill and Lumiansky.

However, Chaucer's importance as a contemporary role model was superseded in the seventeenth and eighteenth centuries by his importance as a historical precedent.[30] It is a truism that between the Middle Ages and modern times, the European sense of identity has shifted from clan to nation. In the Middle Ages, community was essentially tribal. What we now think of as England, France, Germany, or Italy were welters of local city-states and dukedoms dominated by now one overlord and now another. The all-embracing bond, the residue of six centuries of domination by the Roman Empire, was the Roman church. The "fellow" was the Christian, the "alien" was the pagan. The Renaissance was characterized by the disintegration of the notion of the "Holy Roman Empire" and the rise of secular nation states, in which the demise of international Latin and the emergence of vernacular national languages played an important part. The fellow became the compatriot who spoke the same language and the alien the foreigner who spoke another language. The sixteenth and seventeenth centuries were the period during which these national identities began to be fashioned throughout Europe.

The historical view of the English language began with the Tudor movement to establish the distinctiveness of the English Church. This was inspired largely by Matthew Parker, Archbishop of Canterbury (1562–1575). Parker justified the break with Rome by arguing that it was a return to the purity of the primitive Anglo-Saxon church. To secure evidence, he began collecting English documents dating from before the papal ascendancy, and in so doing created a climate in which advancement in both church and state could be assisted by scholarship in Anglo-Saxon. He himself edited King Alfred's preface to Pope Gregory's *Pastoral Care,* which advocated translation of ecclesiastical documents into English; he supported the Anglo-Saxon studies of such scholars as Laurence Nowell and William Lambarde; he founded the Society of Antiquaries which coordinated exploration into all aspects of English antiquities.[31]

Chaucer was caught up in this movement and was regarded, like King Alfred and Bishop Aelfric, as a forerunner of the Protestant Reformation. His satirical exposure of the corruption of religious orders has been shown by modern scholars to be typical of informed commentary throughout Europe in the fourteenth century, most recently by Penn Szittya in *The Antifraternal Tradition in Medieval Literature,*[32] but at the time of Henry VIII's break with Rome, this criticism was seized upon as support for the antipapal cause. William Thynne, Clerk of the Kitchen to Henry VIII, was encouraged by Henry to undertake the first collected edition of Chaucer's works. In this edition (1532), he wanted to include the anticlerical Plowman's and Pilgrim's Tales, but was advised against it by Henry himself, who said that it would draw down upon him the wrath of the bishops. In his second edition (1542), he did include the Plowman's Tale, which shows how the ethos had shifted in ten years. In that same year Parliament promulgated "An Acte for thavauncement of true Religion and for thabolisshment of the contrarie," providing that all books in English printed before 1540 exhibiting radical Protestant doctrines such as those of Tyndale and the Anabaptists be destroyed. Excepted from this edict were English translations of the Bible other than Tyndale's, royal proclamations, laws, prayers, and "Cronycles, Canterburye tales, Chausers bokes, Gowers bokes, and stories of mennes lieves."[33]

In the second edition of his enormously influential *Ecclesiasticall History* (1570 and six more editions before 1641), John Foxe finessed the purpose of the 1542 statute. Clearly he considered the prohibition too general, but he felt that it did emphasize Chaucer's foreshadowing of Protestantism:

> This I mervell, to see the idle life of the priestes and clergyemen of that tyme, seyng these lay persons [Chaucer and Gower] shewed themselves in these kynde of liberall studies so industrious & fruitfully occupied: but muche more I mervell to consider this, how that the Bishoppes condemnyng and abolishyng al maner of Englishe bookes and treatises, which might bryng the people to any light of knowledge, did yet authorise the woorkes of Chaucer to remayne still & to be occupyed: Who [Chaucer] (no doubt) saw in Religion as much almost, as even we do now, and uttereth in hys works no lesse, and semeth right Wiclevian [Wyclifian], or els was never any, and that all his workes almost, if they be thoroughly advised [examined], will testifie (albeit it bee done in myrth, & covertly) and especially the latter ende of hys thyrd booke of the Testament of love: for there purely he toucheth the highest matter, and that is the Communion. Wherin, excepte a man be altogether blynd, he may espye him at the full [fully, clearly]. Althoughe in the same book (as in all other he useth to do) under shadows covertly, as under a visoure, he suborneth truth, in such sorte, as both prively she may profite the godly-minded, and yet not be espyed of the craftye adversarie. And therfore the Byshops, belike, takyng his workes but for jestes and toyes, in condemnyng other bookes, yet permitted his bookes to be read.[34]

The medieval Church had, indeed, prohibited vernacular translations of the Bible, which were encouraged by the act of 1542 as long as they met the test of orthodoxy. The *Testament of Love* by Thomas Usk, discussed before in connection with Chaucer's reputation during his lifetime, was printed as Chaucer's in Thynne's edition and accepted by all editors until Skeat unraveled the Usk acrostic in his 1892 Oxford edition.

In his exposition, Foxe compared Chaucer and Gower to Linacre and Pace as forerunners of the Reformation, and he reprinted "A treatise of Geoffrey Chawser intituled *Jacke Uplande*." This was a series of sixty-four rabidly antifraternal questions by the "hillbilly" (Jack Upland) about the friars' lifestyle and world view that closely resemble the characterizations of friars in *Canterbury Tales*. This propaganda, dated in Joseph Wright's *Political Poems* about 1401, had been attributed to Chaucer and given royal imprimatur in a version "Prynted for John Gough, cum Privilegio Regali," printed between 1536 and 1540, and was included in Speght's edition of Chaucer. Although eliminated from the canon by Tyrwhitt, it was as late as 1835 still defended as Chaucer's by Charles Cowden-Clarke.[35]

Spurgeon records many other sixteenth-century allusions to Chaucer as a forerunner of the Reformation and as a theologian. These were reinforced by Chaucer's reputation for learning that began in his own lifetime with Deschamps's reference to him as "Socrates plains de philosophie" and Thomas Usk's as "the noble philosophical poete in Englissh." Lydgate seems to have been more impressed by Chaucer's style than by his learning, but Hoccleve terms him "mirour of fructuous entendement [meaning] / universal fadir in science," and this became a familiar characterization, reemphasized by Sir Brian Tuke in the introduction to Thynne's edition.[36] Chaucer's broad range over Latin, French, and Italian authors, and from the fabliaux through all the other narrative genres to theology, philosophy, and astronomy still strikes us as remarkable, and it was particularly important during the period in which English was seeking to assert its legitimacy as a vehicle for sophisticated expression. And to the attributes of eloquence and learning was joined another, not unrelated to his reputation as a moral reformer.

Until Dryden, Chaucer was regarded as the poet of love par excellence. This, too, began in his lifetime, with Usk's encomiums in *The Testament of Love* and in Deschamps's testimony, "Tu es d'amours mondains dieux en Albie"[37] ("Thou art a mundane god of love in Albion"), and especially when John Gower had Venus bid the dreamer at the end of *Confessio Amantis*

> Adieu, for I mot fro the wende.
> And gret wel Chaucer whan ye mete,
> As mi disciple [that is, disciple of Venus] and mi poete:
> For in the floures of his youthe
> In sondri wise, as he wel couthe,
> Of ditees and of songes glade,
> The whiche he for mi sake made,
> The lond fulfild is overal:
> Wherof to him in special
> Above alle othre I am most holde [indebted].[38]

This view of Chaucer as the poet of love, reiterated in so many early allusions, explains the popularity of *Troylus and Criseyde*. Until 1700 this piece was considered Chaucer's principal achievement, much more important than the *Canterbury Tales*. Gower refers to the story in his French poem *Mirour de l'homme* (c. 1380), as does the anonymous *Gest hystoriale of the destruction of Troy* (c. 1400). Although these references may be to the Latin or Italian versions of the story, they seem to reflect the influence of Chaucer's handling. As Spurgeon points out, up to 1700 there are twice as many references to *Troylus* as to the *Canterbury Tales,* and three times as many as to the General Prologue. Henryson wrote a sequel to it (1475). Berthelette in the foreword to his edition of *Confessio Amantis* (1532) called it Chaucer's "most special warke." It is the poem Sidney knew best: "Chaucer, undoubtedly did excellently in hys *Troylus and Cressid;* of whom, truly I know not, whether to mervaile more, either that he in that mistie time, could see so clearly, or that wee in this cleare age, walke so stumblingly after him."[39] Spenser based his Spenserian stanza upon its verse form. Shakespeare provided his own critique of courtly love in his adaptation of the Knight's Tale in *Two Gentlemen of Verona* (1598), and of *Troylus* itself in *Troilus and Cressida* (1602).[40] The plot of the first three books was adapted in *Sir Giles Gooscappe* (1606) as a "comedie presented by the Children of the Chappell." In 1630 Jonathan Sidnam published the first modernization of any of Chaucer's poems, *A Paraphrase upon the three first Bookes of Chaucer's Troilus and Cressida Translated into our Moderne English For the satisfaction of those Who either cannot, or will not take ye paines to understand The Excellent Authors Farr more Exquisite and significant Expressions Though now growen obsolete, and out of use,* and in 1635 Sir Francis Kynaston sought to preserve the poem for posterity by publishing a Latin translation, *Amorum Troili et Cressidae libri duo priores Anglico-Latini.*[41]

In the first chapter and at the beginning of the previous chapter we supported the view that courtly love was such a universal theme in medieval society because it came to be regarded as a culture marker, the quality that distinguished the gentle from the churl. Courtly love continued to play this role in English aristocratic society until the Puritan Revolution of 1642. In the royal court of the Tudors, proper appreciation of the refining effects of love was as important to the aspiring courtier as proper clothes or proper manners. Even more than the courtiers of Edward III and Richard II, the courtiers of Henry VIII and Elizabeth were expected to understand and write about love.[42] Henry and Elizabeth themselves composed love songs and poems. George Puttenham in *The Arte of English Poesie* (1589) refers to the "crew of Courtly makers, Noble men and Gentlemen of her Majesties owene servauntes, who have written excellently well," and cites Wyatt, Surrey, Sidney, Raleigh, Dyer, Fulk-Greville, Gascon, Britton, Tuberville "and many other learned Gentlemen. . . . But of them all particularly this is myne opinion, that Chaucer, with Gower, Lidgat and Harding for their antiquitie ought to have the first place, and Chaucer as the most renowmed of them all, for the much learning appeareth to be in him above any of the rest." Spenser's poems of governorship through pastoral and heroic love were cynosures of Elizabethan high culture. And writing love poetry continued as a mark of qualification with Caroline poets, both those in the government and those, like Donne, Herbert, and Vaughn, who wrote for the court even though for various reasons they could not be entirely of it.

Chaucer as a poet of love was father to the courtly ideal as it shaded from the aristocratic into the genteel tradition: the patronizing Victorian and BBC1 tradition in which art is intended to indoctrinate the lower classes in the values and behavior of the gentility. The "moral" tales in the Canterbury collection and *Troylus and Criseyde* served this end. Chaucer's fabliaux were known and deplored. In sermons by clerics like Bishop Hugh Latimer and Archbishop Thomas Cranmer (both in 1549), a "Canterbury tale" is a term for something vulgar and demeaning. As Latimer expressed it, "if good lyfe do not insue and follow upon our readynge to the example of others we myghte as well spende that tyme in reading of prophane hystories, or canterbury tales, or a fit [an episode] of Roben Hode." The reactions of the genteel tradition to the naturalistic element in Chaucer's oeuvre lasted from the sixteenth century until the twentieth. There is a continuity between the demurral that Sir John Harington prefixed to his translation of *Orlando Furioso* (1591) and Robert Kilburn Root's in *The Poetry of Chaucer* (1922):

> [Harington] [Me] thinks I can smile at the fitness of some that will condemne him [Ariosto], and yet not onely allow, but admire our *Chawcer,* who both in worde & sence, incurreth far more the reprehension of flat scurrilitie, as I could recite many places, not onely in his millers tale, but in the good wife of Bathes tale, & many more, in which onely the decorum he keepes is that excuseth it, and maketh it more tolerable.

> [Root] Inasmuch as the *Canterbury Tales* are in the main truly great art, and as these tales [the fabliaux] are by their nature not true

art, I think it unfortunate that Chaucer included them; but I am very far from considering them as evidence of the immoral character of their author.

But as the twentieth century has progressed, the view of the fabliaux has shifted to the point where Derek Brewer could opine in 1968, "It has reasonably been suggested that these indecent anecdotes were Chaucer's greatest interest in his maturity. Indecent as they are, their fundamental morality has been emphasized. Furthermore, they are now accepted as among Chaucer's highest achievements."[43]

After 1660 the court came less and less to set the tone for English culture and, as has always been the case, another facet of Chaucer's achievement began to claim attention. With Dryden, Pope, and Swift, literature turned from presenting morality as an aristocratic virtue to presenting it as a Puritan virtue expected of all classes and all individuals.[44] In previous chapters I distinguished between satire and complaint. Complaint is the medieval, moralistic genre of sober criticism of the ways in which members of the estates fall short of performing the functions established for them in a Platonic world view. Satire is the classical and modern ridicule of individual actions in terms of an Aristotelian, behavioristic world view. The sixteenth-century divines regarded Chaucer as a moral poet of complaint and cited his denunciation of sins of the estates, such as dice and cards (Ascham, 1544), evils of the friars (Foxe, 1570), the "knaverie of Incubus" (Scott, 1584), and worshiping false relics (Letter from a Parliamentary officer, 1645).[45] William Webbe's perceptive remarks in *A Discourse of English Poetry* (1586) are characteristic of the view of Chaucer as a poet of complaint:

> He by his delightsome vayne, so gulled the eares of men with his devises, that, although corruption bare such a sway in most matters, that learning and truth might skant bee admitted to shewe it selfe, yet without controllment [restraint] myght he gyrde at the vices and abuses of all states, and gawle [puncture] with very sharpe and eger inventions, which he did so learnedly and pleasantly, that none therefore would call him into question.[46]

Criticism of the "vices and abuses of all the [e]states" is very differ-ent from creation of individual characters that has since Eric Auerbach's influential book come to be designated "mimesis."[47] The critic who popularized the mimetic quality of Chaucer's art was John Dryden. His criticism in *Fables Ancient and Modern* (1700) replaced appreciation of Chaucer's moralism with appreciation of his realism and dramatic art.[48] After 1700, *Canterbury Tales,* especially the General Prologue, replaced *Troylus and Criseyde* as Chaucer's principal accomplishment, and even *Troylus and Criseyde* was reevaluated as "the first English novel" instead of as an exemplification of courtly decorum. This was in keeping with the emergence of the realistic novel. Since 1700 until the 1950s (I will discuss the reemergence of moral and social criticism below), Chaucer's stories have been read more for their dramatic vividness than for their moral instruction. In a very real sense, it has been the English novelists like Fielding, Jane Austen, and Dickens, not the poets like Pope, Keats, and Tennyson, who profited most from the realistic characterization and psychological interaction in the *Canterbury Tales* and *Troylus.*

Dryden regarded Chaucer's accomplishment as narrative rather than sententious. His *Fables* are translations from four classic fabulists—Homer, Ovid, Boccaccio, and Chaucer—all of whom he describes as creators of their respective languages but especially as story tellers. Dryden begins his discussion of Chaucer with the first substantive comparisons ever made of the similarities between the narrative tech-niques of Chaucer, Ovid, and Boccaccio, all of whom, he says, "under-stood the Manners; under which name I comprehend the Passions, and, in a larger sense, the Descriptions of Persons." After a very keen critical analysis he gives the palm to Chaucer:

> [Chaucer] must have been a Man of a most wonderful comprehensive
> Nature, because, as it has been truly observ'd of him, he has taken
> into the Compass of his *Canterbury Tales* the various Manners and
> Humours (as we now call them) of the whole *English* nation, in his
> Age. Not a single Character has escap'd him. All his Pilgrims are
> severally [individually] distinguish'd from each other; and not only in

their Inclinations, but in their very Phisiognomies and Persons. *Baptista Porta* could not have describ'd their Natures better, than by the Marks which the Poet gives them. The Matter and Manner of their Tales, and of their Telling, are so suited to their different Educations, Humours, and Callings, that each of them would be improper in any other Mouth. Even the grave and serious Characters are distinguish'd by their several sorts of Gravity: Their Discourses are such as belong to their Age, their Calling, and their Breeding; such as are becoming of them, and of them only. Some of his Persons are Vicious, and some Virtuous; some are unlearn'd, or (as *Chaucer* calls them) Lewd, and some are Learn'd. Even the Ribaldry of the Low Characters is different: the *Reeve,* the *Miller,* and the *Cook,* are several [individual] Men, and are distinguish'd from each other, as much as the mincing Lady-Prioress, and the broad-speaking, gap-toothed Wife of *Bathe.*

Modern discussion of Chaucer's realism has not got much further than this. Dryden was the first critic to emphasize the emergence of the individual in Chaucer's poetry and his judgment has either directly or indirectly provided the basis for all later criticism.

Dryden did, however, have his blind spots about Chaucer. Although he spoke of him repeatedly as a creator of the English language, he did not understand that the differences in Chaucer's English represent historical patterns of grammar and pronunciation. He regarded the differences simply as mistakes: Chaucer was "a rough Diamond, and must first be polish'd e're he shines." The distinction between "modern" and "ancient" culture had begun to be recognized in the Renaissance; the first *OED* citation to this meaning of "modern" is by Dunbar in 1520. But that definition lumped everything postclassical as modern—as in the "Modern Language Association of America," most of whose concerns were until recently medieval. The notion of a middle period between the classical and modern, with its own patterns of language and behavior, began to emerge in the eighteenth century. Latin *medium aevum* is cited from 1604; the first *OED* citation to "middle ages" as a historical period is 1722. But recognition of older forms of the vernacular languages did not come for another hundred years. Even Tyrwhitt, who did view Chaucer historically, could not deal with his pronunciation (except the final *e*) or accidence. This understanding was left for the historical grammarians in the nineteenth century, particularly in the case of Chaucer to Francis J. Child of Harvard University, whose "Observations on the Language of Chaucer" in the *Memoires of the American Academy* (1862) provided the first accessible analysis of his pronunciation and grammar (there had, indeed, been a Bonn dissertation on the subject in 1847, upon which Child drew). But throughout the seventeenth and eighteenth centuries, Dryden and his contemporaries felt fully justified in "improving" the archaic or provincial language of a "modern" colleague.

Even more interesting is Dryden's blindness to Chaucer's satire and irony. Particularly curious is his failure to emphasize the satire, which he did recognize. Satire had become a recognized genre with Gascoigne, Hall, Nash, and others in the English Renaissance. Dryden himself wrote satires, observing in the address to the reader in *Hind & Panther* that "the commonplaces of *satire* . . . are not my invention but as old, to my knowledge, as the times of Boccace and Chaucer on the one side, and those of the Reformation on the other."[49] In discussing Chaucer's religion in the *Fables,* Dryden accepted John Foxe's interpretation of Chaucer as a moralist with "some little Byas towards the Opinions of Wicliff." He defends his own criticism both of government and the church, concluding "I have followed *Chaucer,* in his Character of a Holy Man, and have enlarg'd on that subject with some Pleasure, reserving to myself the Right, if I shall think fit hereafter, to describe other sorts of Priests, such as are more easily to be found than the Good Parson."

What is lacking in Dryden's critique is any recognition at all of Chaucer's humor. Indeed, he rates Chaucer as superior to Ovid because he is more serious. Sober criticism—preaching—is the stuff of complaint; humorous criticism—ridicule, parody—is the stuff of satire. Dryden had indulged in heavy-handed ridicule in his own satires like *Absolom and Achitophel* and *Mac Flecknoe,* but he did not perceive satiric humor in Chaucer. He translated only the Knight's Tale, the Wife of Bath's Tale (not her prologue), the Nun's Priest's Tale, the Character of the Good Parson, and the spurious "Flower and Leaf," all of which presented Chaucer as a courtly and moralistic poet rather than as a satirist. "I have confined my Choice to such Tales of *Chaucer* as savour nothing of Immodesty," he says. He quotes Chaucer's defense of his "broad speaking" in the General Prologue (1.725–42), yet ends with the demurral that continued into the generation of Root and John M. Manly: "Yet if a man should have inquired of *Boccoce* or of *Chaucer,* what need they had of introducing such Characters, when obscene Words were proper to their mouths, but very undecent to be heard; I know not what Answer they could have made. For that Reason, such Tales shall be left untold by me."

Other, but far less influential, critics did refer to Chaucer's writings as "merry," "witty," and "jovial," but until our own generation, these have tended to be deprecatory judgments. Spurgeon, in her discussion of the allusions to Chaucerian humor, observes that Thomas Warton (1754) recognized Chaucer as the first English writer to possess humor in the modern sense. Leigh Hunt in his anthology *Wit and Humour, Selected from the English Poets* (1846), appreciated that "Chaucer's comic genius is so perfect, that it may be said to include prophetic intimations of all that followed it," but he bowdlerized, just as Dryden had, apologizing, "I wish I could have given more than one comic story out of Chaucer; but the change of manners renders it difficult at any time, and impossible in a book like the present."[50] And two pages later, "When Chaucer is free from the taint of his age [that is, coarseness], his humour is of a description the most thoroughly delightful." Matthew Arnold gave the coup de grace of the Victorian Age to Chaucer's humor when he refused to include him among the poets of the first rank because he lacked the "high seriousness of the great classics,"[51] and this impression, reinforced by his reputation for coarseness and ribaldry, lasted through the first half of the twentieth century, as witnessed by the bowdlerizing of J. M. Manly's edition of *Canterbury Tales* (1928)[52] and the apology of Robert K. Root cited above.

What Chaucer has been most valued for from 1700 until the present is the realism praised in the passage from Dryden quoted above. The qualities that made the *Canterbury Tales* a cynosure for modern literature is perfectly expressed by Erich Auerbach's famous contrast between the mimetic values of epic and Scripture: on the one hand, the Homeric style of externalized and uniformly illuminated phenomena, at a definite time and in a definite place, in a perpetual foreground; on the other hand, the Biblical style placed emphasis on only the decisive points of the narrative; what lies between is nonexistent; the whole remains mysterious and "frought with background."[53] Both of these values appear in *Canterbury Tales,* and to a lesser extent in Chaucer's other poems. The externalized phenomena are the realistic details, dialogue, and actions—not excepting the actuality of the poet persona himself. The mystery and sense of background are produced by Chaucer's silences and the incompletenesses and disorganization of the texts—the impossibility of pinning down any detail or structure, and yet the tantalizing aura of unity and purpose that surrounds the apparent whole.

In previous chapters, we have observed that Chaucer's extension of the subject matter of literature beyond the interests of the royal courts to the interests of the inns of court and the merchant pui is one of his important contributions. The appreciation of Chaucer's noncourtly realism reflects the changed audience for literature since 1700 as much as it does Chaucer's own audiences. Many critics have pointed out that the medieval courtly romances and allegories of the court of love of Chaucer and the French court poets are quite realistic presentations of the settings, behavior, and ideals of medieval aristocratic society. But that society represented perhaps three or four percent of the total population. Since 1700, the literary public has expanded to include a much larger middle class and proletariat. Along with the expansion of the public has come the extension of the idea of realism to include language and behavior that the genteel tradition proscribed as uncourteous (that is, etymologically, "uncourtly"). This extension to treatment of the impolite and uncourteous has been termed naturalism.

The tension between the genteel and the naturalistic is mirrored in the attitude towards Chaucer's fabliaux. As we have observed, until well after 1900 this genre was virtually ignored. The first collection of the French fabliaux was that of Anatole de Montaiglon and Gaston Raynaud completed in 1890, and the first critical study that of Joseph Bédier in 1893.[54] The first study of the relationship between the styles and subject matters of Chaucer's polite and naturalistic poems was Charles Muscatine's *Chaucer and the French Tradition* (1957). Only very recently have the obscenities in the language of Chaucer and the French poets begun to be studied.[55]

Both Bédier and Muscatine viewed polite romances and allegories as addressed to the courtly audience and naturalistic fabliaux as addressed to the bourgeois audience. In the same year as Muscatine, Per Nykrog published *Les Fabliaux* (1957), which denied that the romances and fabliaux were addressed to different audiences, but called them simply different styles, addressed to the same audience under different circumstances. In the drawing room the audience would expect idealism and romance; in the drinking room it would expect satire and raunchy humor. The different classes of characters Nykrog explained as stylistic markers. Until the nineteenth century, the genteel tradition reserved the capacity for courtesy and idealism to the genteel classes, and churlish vulgarity to peasant or bourgeois classes. The possibility of treating the loves and sorrows of the lower classes seriously emerged with the realistic writers of the nineteenth century, like Balzac, Zola, Dickens, Bennett, Hardy, and eventually the naturalistic writers like Joyce and D. H. Lawrence, or Crane, Dreiser, James T. Ferrall, and many others. I mention only a few obvious novelists; the same sort of movement is found in the drama and, more recently, in lyric poetry.

Chaucer's pioneering movement towards encompassing both genteel and naturalistic subject matters and styles has probably had little direct influence on the broadening of the scope of literature and art in the last hundred years, but his breadth and the exquisite decorum with which he handled naturalistic details and language must have helped justify the experiments of James Joyce, William Faulkner, and other contemporary writers. At the very least, it has made Chaucer a fellow of the contemporary circle to an even greater extent than Shakespeare or Milton. Because of his language, most of the direct discussion has been academic, but there are now each year nearly as many books and articles explaining the art and meaning of Chaucer's eight fabliaux (twenty-seven items in 1988) as of the other fifteen Canterbury tales (thirty-two in 1988). And all of Chaucer's themes—realistic, romantic, and risqué—continue to be favorites for discussion by all manner of readers.

Until 1700 Chaucer was important as a model for the decorum and sophistication expressed in his genteel poetry. After 1700 he continued to be important for this, but he also became a model for realistic representation of characters and situations. In the twentieth century he has continued to be important both for moralism and realism, but he has also become important for the naturalism of his fabliaux. But since about 1940 it is the multilayeredness of his poetry that has attracted the most attention.

C. S. Lewis's *The Allegory of Love* (1937) was the first popular presentation of medieval literature as multilayered. Until that book, chivalry and courtly love had been accepted as the depiction of a genuine lifestyle, and, indeed, the first chapter of Lewis's book describes the medieval court culture in which the wife of the baron was surrounded by a group of unmarried retainers who vied with one another for her favor. But Lewis looked beneath this familiar scenario and analyzed the process of the love allegories from the *Roman de la Rose* through the *Faerie Queen* as Freudian psychological dramas in which inner conflict was externalized by personifying each drive and emotion as a specific character, and the conflict of the emotions by conflict between the allegorical characters. In *Roman de la Rose* Bialacoil (Fair welcome), Douz Regart (Sweet looking), Franchise (Sincerity), Pity (Kindness), Shame, Danger (Rebuff), and Venus (Sexual desire) are all aspects of the feminine psyche in a courtship situation, as Douz Penser (Sweet thinking), Esperance (Hope), Venus, and especially Raison (Reason) are aspects of the male. There are inner conflicts between the feminine impulses to invite and reject sexual attention, and the masculine impulses to succumb to and reject sexual desire, as well as the eternal conflict between the sexes. Lewis redirected attention to the psychological significance of Chaucer's love poetry after more than two centuries during which it had been viewed only as the least interesting exercise of his narrative realism, satire, and humor. He analyzed Chaucer's short poems as representative of the psychological symbolism of the *Roman de la Rose,* but without its allegorical action. His analysis of *Book of the Duchess* lies behind the psychoanalytic reinterpretations of the poem discussed in chapter 4, and he presents *Troylus and Criseyde* as "the consummation, not the abandonment, of his labors as a poet of courtly love,"[56] an excercise in which the psychological comedy of *Roman de la Rose* is converted into psychological tragedy. As in the *Roman,* the real story of *Troylus* is not the surface actions of Pandarus and the lovers, but the internal conflicts between their desires and fears as externalized in the conventional language and situations of the allegory of love.

Lewis's introduction to reading medieval love allegory as multilayered was extended ten years later by D. W. Robertson, Bernard F. Huppé, and others who built upon the perception that medieval people were constrained by their dualistic theology to view the universe as multilayered.[57] Medieval neo-Platonism was no new discovery, but the Robertsonians argued that in the medieval world view, every external phenomenon and event stood for a theological abstraction. Medieval rhetoric taught that language conveyed meaning by *literatus,* the literal meaning of the words; *sensus,* the obvious sense of the text; and *sententia,* what the communication implied beyond what it literally said. The ultimate goal was to understand the sentence of the text. In turn, sententia encompassed three levels of meaning: *moralis,* the moral meaning in the realm of human experience; *allegoricus,* the allegorical meaning in the realm of human apprehension of the divine; and *anagogicus,* anagogical revelation of the structure of the divine. When Usk said in *Testament of Love* that "in wytte and in good reson of sentence [Chaucer] passeth al other makers," he was calling attention to this dimension of Chaucer's writing.[58]

Medieval commentators developed an elaborate system of allegorical interpretation of the Scriptures and pagan poetry in which moral, allegorical, and anagogical equivalents were systematically noted for every phenomenon in the material world—plants, animals, colors, seasons, jewels, and so forth ad infinitum. Lay poets like Dante purported to write on the four levels of literal, moral, allegorical, and anagogical meaning. And a lively discussion has grown up since 1950 within the academy about the extent to which Chaucer and all other medieval literature can be interpreted in the light of the Patristic levels of meaning.[59]

However the specifics of the methodology of Lewis and the Robertsonians may be regarded, their criticism introduced into the interpretation of Chaucer and other medieval literature an awareness that medieval writers were capable of saying one thing and meaning another. This has blossomed in the last quarter century into great sensitivity to the multilayered meaning of medieval writing, a sensitivity almost totally lacking before 1950.[60] Sensitivity to multiple meanings has reinforced awareness of another of Chaucer's special attributes, the multilayeredness of the Chaucerian voices. This aspect of Chaucer's style was recognized by the Puritan commentators, but largely ignored from Dryden through Kittredge, Manly, and Lowes. During this period of concentration on mimesis, Chaucer and all other medieval poets seem to have been taken at face value, moralistic if sententious, simply entertaining if humorous. But there are many references by Foxe and others in the sixteenth century to the "covert" manner in which Chaucer's "pleasant wit" and "merry tales" attacked corruption. Thomas Lodge says (1579) that "*Chaucer* in pleasant vain can rebuke sin uncontrold; &

though he be lavish in the letter, his sence is serious." William Webbe
says (1586), "For such was his bolde spyrit, that the enormities he saw
in any, he would not spare to pay them home, eyther in playne words,
or els in some prety and pleasant covert, that the simplest might espy
him."[61] This awareness of a serious purpose behind the realism and
humor seems to have been lost for nearly three centuries, to be revived
after the middle of the twentieth century.[62]

Chaucer the social critic, Chaucer the ironist, may be as much the
creation of contemporary readership as of authorial intention. But as
we sum up the importance of Chaucer, the miracle is how well his poetry
lends itself to twentieth-century social and psychological literary theory,
as it did to the mimetic literary theory of the eighteenth and nineteenth
centuries and to the moralistic literary theory of the sixteenth and seventeenth. Recognition of different levels of Chaucer's meaning is admirably
suited to modern psychological criticism. The narrative level that simply
describes a character or tells a story and the ironic level that subverts the
obvious meaning are both really there, waiting to be perceived.

The ambiguity of Chaucer's style and language is a supreme example
of the way that modern narrative seeks to involve the reader in the
process of inferring, deciding, and evaluating. This is one of the qualities
that makes Chaucerian narrative so convincing. The incomplete texts
and the variety of their presentations in the manuscripts lend themselves
to the stream-of-consciousness techniques of Virginia Woolf, James
Joyce, and William Faulkner in which the reader must weave together
the various strands in an effort to achieve a coherent pattern. What
Browning strives to create through the multiple voices of *The Ring and
the Book* and Faulkner in the multiple voices of *The Sound and the Fury*
are implicit in the multiple voices and amorphous structure of the
Canterbury Tales.

In particular, the richness and variety that enable a Terry Jones to
argue that the Knight and his tale (which have always been read as a
celebration of chivalry) are satire on the decline of chivalry,[63] and Judson
Allen to argue that the Parson's tale (which has been read as expression

of orthodox religion) is satire on the ideas of penance and absolution,[64] and Elaine Hansen to argue that *Legend of Good Women* (which has always been read as typical medieval antifeminism) is a parody on anti-feminism,[65] represent the universality that gives immortality to all of the classic authors, Homer or Dante or Shakespeare or Goethe. Like all of these, Chaucer fulfills the expectations of each succeeding generation. But he occupies the unique position in English of having been first in nearly every one of the important qualities. He was the first to use cultivated London English for sophisticated poetry, and the first to use English prose for science and philosophy. Chaucer was the first to use cultivated English to express love as decorum and psychological allegory. Chaucer was the first to extend the scope of poetry beyond courtly manners and religion to humanism and naturalism. Chaucer was the first to recognize himself and to be recognized as an author, and the first to create through language psychologically realistic plots and characters. He was the first English writer systematically to employ humor, satire, and irony to imply serious criticism of behavior and ideas under the guise of simple entertainment.

Chaucer's influence as a model probably ended with Spenser, but awareness of his precedence and prescience has informed English poetry and the English novel from the seventeenth century onward. To modern readers, perhaps his greatest service is as evidence of the impossibility of translation. The same is no doubt true of Homer and all other great writers. But Chaucer's language is just close enough so that most readers can with only a little effort grasp the meaning and effect of his original expression and feel the raising of the hairs on the back of the neck that is the proof of perfect poetic expression. "Whan that Aprill with his shoures soote / The droghte of March hath perced to the roote" is so incomparably superior to "When April has pierced the drouth of March to the roots with its sweet showers" that there is nothing more to say.

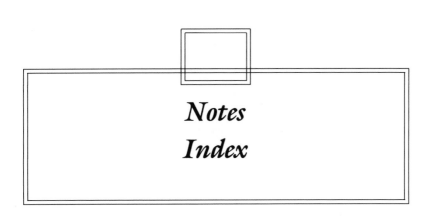

Notes
Index

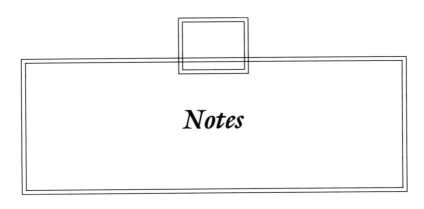

Notes

BD *Book of the Duchess,*
    1369
PF *Parliament of Fowls,*
    1377
HF *House of Fame,* 1380
    or 1381
Boece, between 1381 and 1385
TC *Troylus and Criseyde,*
    between 1382 and 1385
LGW *Legend of Good
    Women,* 1385 or 1386
CT *Canterbury Tales,*
    begun in 1386
*Astrolabe Treatise on the
    Astrolabe,* 1391
*Equatorie Equatorie of the
    Planets,* 1392

Gen Pro General
    Prologue
KT Knight's Tale
MilT Miller's Tale
RvT Reeve's Tale
CkT Cook's Tale
MLT Man of Law's Tale
WBP Wife of Bath's
    Prologue
WBT Wife of Bath's Tale
FrT Friar's Tale
SumT Summoner's Tale
CIT Clerk's Tale
MerchT Merchant's Tale
SqT Squire's Tale
FrankT Franklin's Tale
PardT Pardoner's Tale

PhysT Physicians's Tale
ShipT Shipman's Tale
PrioressT Prioress's Tale
*Thopas Tale of Sir Thopas
Mel Tale of Melibee*
MkT Monk's Tale
NPT Nun's Priest's Tale
2ndNT Second Nun's
    Tale
CYT Canon's Yeoman's
    Tale
MancT Manciple's Tale
ParsT Parson's Tale
Ret Retraction

Preface

1. Thomas Speght's "Life of Chaucer" in *Chaucer's Works* (1598) is conveniently reprinted by Eleanor Prescott Hammond, *Chaucer: A Bibliographical Manual* (New York: Macmillan, 1908) 24ff. Russell Krauss, "Chaucerian Problems: Especially the Petherton Forestership and the Question of Thomas Chaucer," in *Three Chaucer Studies,* ed. Carleton Brown (Oxford UP, 1932) collects the data. J. M. Manly's refutation of Krauss's argument, on the basis of the 1396 suit by Ralph Barton (discussed in chap. 1), *Review of English Studies* 10 (1934): 262–67, and the negative reactions of the many reviews of Krauss (cited in D. D. Griffith, *Bibliography of Chaucer 1908–1953* [U of Washington P, 1955] 15) are summed up by Donald Howard, *Chaucer: His Life, His Work, His World* (New York: Dutton, 1987) 94–95. Howard dismisses the suggestions about Chaucer's unhappy marriage as scandalous gossip, but has to allow at the end, "All are guesses; none can be ruled out."

2. Speght's statement (Hammond, *A Bibliographical Manual* 22) was at once questioned by Francis Thynne, *Animadversions,* ed. F. J. Furnivall, Chaucer Society, 2d Ser. 13 (1876) 21, on the grounds that the Inner Temple was not a

functioning law society until the latter days of Edward III (that is, in the mid-1370s) by which time Chaucer was already Controller of Customs and otherwise established in his professional life. But the Temple was rented to the lawyers in 1324, and the idea that Chaucer was educated there had some currency through the time of Edith Rickert, "Was Chaucer a Student in the Inner Temple?" *Manly Anniversay Studies* (U of Chicago P, 1923) 20–31, and J. M. Manly, ed., *The Canterbury Tales* (New York: Holt, 1928) 12. D. S. Bland's demurral, "Chaucer and the Inns of Court: A Re-examination," *English Studies* 33 (1952): 145–55, makes the same sort of objections as Francis Thynne's. Bland's caution is documented by S. E. Thorne, "The Early History of the Inns of Court with Special Reference to Gray's Inn," *Graya* 50 (1959): 79–96, and E. W. Ives, *The Common Lawyer. Thomas Kebell: A Case Study* (Cambridge UP, 1983) esp. 39ff. But these discussions turn largely on the question of *institutionalized* education in the inns of court, that is, lectures on law and moot courts.

3. Bland, "Chaucer and the Inns of Court" 148, 154.

4. T. F. Tout in a series of studies gives specific information about the apprentice-type situations of the inns of chancery in Chaucer's youth, which I have summarized and cited in chap. 2. The only question is when was this type of education extended to the inns of court? Bland and Thorne feel that Fortescue was extrapolating backward a hundred years the situation of the inns of court in mid fifteenth century, but the introduction to *The Records of the Honorable Society of Lincoln's Inn*, vol. 1 (Lincoln's Inn, 1896) vii, states that Fortescue was a governor of Lincoln's Inn for the first time in 1425, and had been a student at the Inn before 1420. Fortescue's description of the inns, presumably written in the 1460s, often cited but seldom quoted, that I reproduce in toto in chap. 2, gives no indication that the arrangements in the inns had changed in his lifetime, so it must describe a situation somewhat closer to that in Chaucer's youth in the 1360s than Bland and Thorne allow. I wish to thank Mark Allen for information on the evolution in the inns of court and of chancery.

5. *The Oxford Companion to Law*, ed. David M. Walker (Oxford: Clarendon, 1980) s.v. "Inns of Court."

6. Thomas F. Kuhn, *The Structure of Scientific Revolution*, 2d ed. (U of Chicago P, 1970) 2, states: "Concerned with scientific development, the historian then appears to have two main tasks. On the one hand, he must determine by what man and at what point in time each contemporary scientific fact, law, and theory was discovered or invented. On the other, he must describe and explain the congeries of error, myth, and superstition that have inhibited the more rapid accumulation of the constitutents of the modern science text." He then proceeds to discuss how the innovative scientists, Galileo, Newton, Lavoisier, and others, introduced new scientific perceptions by individually "solving puzzles." Cultural change seems to me to proceed in the same way, although it is harder to identify the innovative individuals. I think that Henry V was one of them.

7. Information on the part played by Henry V in the formation of Chancery English is found in J. H. Fisher, "Chancery and the Emergence of Standard Written English in the Fifteenth Century," *Speculum* 52 (1977): 870–99; Malcolm Richardson, "Henry V, the English Chancery, and Chancery English," *Speculum* 55 (1980): 726–50; and J. H. Fisher, Malcolm Richardson, and J. L. Fisher, *An Anthology of Chancery English* (U of Tennessee P, 1984).

8. I have made a start towards assembling information about the creation

of the Ellesmere and other early manuscripts of the *Canterbury Tales* in "Animadversions on the Text of Chaucer, 1988," *Speculum* 63 (1988): 779–93. I add further information in chap. 5.

1. Chaucer and the Emergence of English

1. On Latin and the vernaculars, Philippe Wolff, *Western Languages, A.D. 100–1500,* trans. F. Partridge (London: Wiedenfeld, 1971).

2. On the imperial language and the Roman notaries, Bruno Migliorini, *The Italian Language,* trans T. G. Griffith (London: Faber, 1966) chap. 1.

3. On the transition from orality to literacy, Wolff, *Western Languages* 88ff.; M. T. Clanchey, *From Memory to Written Record* (London: Arnold, 1978).

4. On Charlemagne and the recognition of the vernaculars, Wolff, *Western Languages,* 118ff.; John T. Waterman, *A History of the German Language* (U of Washington P, 1976) 76ff.

5. On the influence of the medieval chancelleries, J. H. Fisher, "European Chancelleries and the Rise of Standard Languages," *Proceedings of the Illinois Medieval Association* 3 (1986): 1–33.

6. On the *ars dictaminis,* James J. Murphy, *Rhetoric in the Middle Ages* (U of California P, 1974) chap. 5.

7. On the movements toward vernacular literacy, J. H. Fisher, "European Chancelleries" 6ff.

8. On English, French, and Latin in medieval England, A. C. Baugh and Thomas Cabel, *A History of the English Language,* 3rd ed. (New York: Prentice Hall, 1978). The question of when the Anglo-Norman court began to use English as its colloquial has nearly as many opinions as commentators. For example, Kathleen Lambley, *The Teaching and Cultivation of the French Language during Tudor and Stuart Times,* French Ser. no. 3 (University of Manchester, 1920) 4–25, argues that the appearance of French teaching materials in the fourteenth century indicates that the nobility by that time had to be taught French, but Helen Suggett, "The Use of French in England in the Late Middle Ages," *Transactions of the Royal Historical Society,* 4th Ser. no. 28 (1946) 61–63, argues that French continued to be the court colloquial until after Henry V (which casts an interesting light on the scene between Henry and Katherine in Shakespeare's *Henry V,* 5.2). Richard Firth Green, *Poets and Princepleasers* (U of Toronto P, 1980) 10, 77ff., takes no position on the court colloquial but shows how completely court education and literature were in French. Paul Strohm, *Social Chaucer* (Harvard UP, 1989) chap. 3, argues, as I do, that Chaucer addressed an audience of equals. He has an excellent bibliographical note (204n.14) on the continued use of French in the court circle. Clearly this is not a question of absolutes; use of English by the aristocracy and middle class must have differed with families and individuals. The real distinction is that all official *writing* was in French and Latin until after the time of Henry V.

9. On the court of Edward III, Paul Johnson, *The Life and Times of Edward III* (London: Weidenfeld, 1973); Juliet Vale, *Edward III and Chivalry* (Cambridge: Brewer, 1982).

10. On the arguments for using English in Parliament, J. H. Fisher, "Chancery and the Emergence of Standard English in the Fifteenth Century" 79–80.

11. On the court of Richard II, Gervase Matthew, *The Court of Richard II* (London: John Murray, 1968).

12. John Gower, *Works,* ed. G. C. Macaulay, vol. 2 (Oxford: Clarendon, 1901) 4–5. Sir John Froissart, *Chronicles,* trans. John Bourchier, Lord Berners. Reprinted from Pynson's ed. 1523, 1525 (London: Rivington, 1812) 2.619.

13. On Henry V and the standardizing of written English, Richardson, "Henry V and the English Chancery" 726–50; J. H. Fisher, Introduction, *Anthology of Chancery English.*

14. On Caxton and Chancery English, J. H. Fisher, "Caxton and Chancery English," in *Fifteenth-Century Studies,* ed. Robert F. Yeager (Hamden, CT: Archon, 1984) 161–85.

15. On the Viking influence and pidginization, Baugh and Cabel, *History,* chap. 4 (which does not use the term but describes the process); Robert McCrum, William Cran, and Robert McNeil, *The Story of English* (New York: Viking, 1986) 68ff. (which does use the term).

16. On the Middle English dialect situation, Baugh and Cabel, *History* 148ff. (very briefly); Kenneth Sisam, *Fourteenth Century Verse and Prose* (Oxford UP, 1968) 265ff. (in more detail).

17. The records are printed and analyzed, with full bibliography, by M. M. Crow and Clair Olson, *Chaucer Life Records* (Oxford: Clarendon, 1966). The most recent effort to set the records in context and form a biography is by Donald R. Howard, *Chaucer.*

18. On Chaucer's education and the St. Paul's school library, Edith Rickert, "Chaucer at School," *Modern Philology* 29 (1932): 257–74.

19. Quotations from Trevisa's 1385 translation of the *Polychronicon* are modernized from Baugh and Cabel, *History* 149–50.

20. On the innovations by Cornwall and Pencrich, W. H. Stevenson, "The Introduction of English as the Vehicle of Instruction in English Schools," *Furnivall Miscellany* (Oxford UP, 1921) 421–29. On the introduction of English studies after the eighteenth century, D. J. Palmer, *The Rise of English Studies* (Oxford UP, 1965) esp. chap. 1.

21. Sir Philip Sidney, "The Defence of Poetry," in *Complete Works,* ed. Albert Feuillerat, vol. 3 (Cambridge UP, 1923) 44.

22. Jonathan Nicholls, *The Matter of Courtesy: Medieval Courtesy Books and the Gawain Poet* (Cambridge: Brewer, 1985) Part 1, explores the nonromantic tradition of courtesy; Green, *Poets and Princepleasers* 82–83, discusses the use of courtesy books in courtly education.

23. Roger Boase, *The Origin and Meaning of Courtly Love* (Manchester UP, 1977) is a bibliographical survey of writing about courtly love in all the European languages from the Middle Ages to about 1975.

24. Nicholls, *The Matter of Courtesy* 7.

25. The ideas of Adams, de Rougemont, Köhler, and others are summarized by Boase, *The Origin and Meaning of Courtly Love.*

26. Laura Kendrick, "The Art of Mastering Servitude: Eustach Deschamps' Deployment of Courtly Love," unpublished paper. Kendrick has developed Köhler's ideas in the first two chapters of *The Game of Love: Troubadour Word Play* (U of California P, 1988).

27. Roger Ascham, "The Scolemaster," in *English Works,* ed. William A. Wright (Cambridge UP, 1904) 231.

28. Jean Froissart, *Chronicles,* trans. Thomas Johnes, vol. 1 (London, Routledge, 1868) 1.

29. The idea of a "religion" of courtly love was evidently first advanced by Eduard Wechssler, *Das kulturproblem des Minnesang* (Halle, 1919). Johan Huizinga in both *The Waning of the Middle Ages,* trans. F. Hopman (1924; New York: Penguin, 1955) and *Homo Ludens,* trans. George Steiner (1944; London: Paladion, 1970) treated courtly love as an elaborate game by which the knightly class veiled reality in a vision of harmonious beauty. Alexander Denomy, *The Heresy of Courtly Love* (Gloucester, MA: Peter Smith, 1965) 35, discusses the substitution of the theological virtues faith, hope, and charity by the courtly virtues *cortesia, proeza, mesure, pretz, valors,* and *jovens* in Andreas Capellanus's *De Amore.*

30. Part 2 of Nicholls, *The Matter of Courtesy* is devoted to the treatment of courtesy in the four *Gawain* poems.

31. On Thomas Chaucer, Martin B. Ruud, *Thomas Chaucer,* University of Minnesota Studies in Language and Literature no. 9 (1926); A. C. Baugh, "Kirk's Life Records of Thomas Chaucer," *PMLA* 47 (1932): 461–515; Crow and Olson, *Chaucer Life Records* 541–44. The *Dictionary of National Biography* gives a substantial listing of Thomas's many grants and offices, and see chap 5. I refer in the Preface to the controversy surrounding Thomas's parentage.

32. I owe the idea that Gaunt would have been guilty of incest if he had bedded both Katherine and Philippa to informative discussions with Henry A. Kelly. But Kelly feels that this is evidence against Gaunt's fathering Thomas while I believe that it could have been the reason contemporaries were so vague about Thomas's parentage.

33. Crow and Olson, *Chaucer Life Records* 541.

34. Crow and Olson, *Chaucer Life Records* 543.

35. Crow and Olson, *Chaucer Life Records* 343–47, with full references.

36. The classic article on Chaucer as a French poet is Rossell Hope Robbins, "Geffroi Chaucier, Poete Francois, Father of English Poetry," *Chaucer Review* 13 (1978): 93–115. See also J. H. Fisher, "Chaucer and French Influence," in *New Perspectives on Chaucer Criticism,* ed. Donald M. Rose (Norman, OK: Pilgrim Books, 1981).

37. James I. Wimsatt, ed., *Chaucer and the Poems of "Ch"* (Cambridge: Brewer, 1982) 10–11.

38. "Womanly Noblesse," short poem no. 7, in J. H. Fisher, *Complete Poetry and Prose* 694. On the authenticity of this poem see George B. Pace and Alfred David, eds., *The Minor Poems of Geoffrey Chaucer, Variorum Chaucer* 1.5 (U of Oklahoma P, 1982) 179–80. The title of this poem is significant, "Noblesse." The non-erotic ideal of nobility fostered by the courtesy tradition—the "truth, honor, freedom, and courtesy" of Chaucer's Knight—is here transferred to the woman.

39. Jean Froissart, *Le Paradis d'Amour, L'Orloge Amoureus,* ed. Peter F. Dembowski (Geneva: Droz, 1986) 40.

40. On the French sources for *Book of the Duchess* see James Wimsatt, *Chaucer and the French Love Poets* (U of North Carolina P, 1968) 155–62.

41. The French and Latin parallels to all but the *Equatorie* are conveniently cited in the *Riverside Chaucer,* ed. Larry D. Benson (Boston: Houghton, 1987).

The sources of the *Equatorie* are treated by J. D. North, *Chaucer's Universe* (Oxford: Clarendon, 1988) chap. 4.

42. On the relations between Chaucer's *Troylus* and the French, Robert A. Pratt, "Chaucer and *La Roman de Troyle et de Criseida*," *Studies in Philology* 53 (1956): 509–39.

43. Wolfgang Clemen, *Chaucer's Early Poetry*, trans. C. A. M. Sym (New York: Barnes and Noble, 1964) 7.

44. Statistics from Joseph Mersand, *Chaucer's Romance Vocabulary* (New York: Comet, 1939). Norman Davis, "Chaucer and Fourteenth-Century English," in *Geoffrey Chaucer: Writers and Their Backgrounds,* ed. Derek Brewer (London: Bell, 1974) does not question the statistics, but he objects to the lack of discrimination in Mersand's number crunching. He stresses that attention must be paid to the status of individual Romance words. He is still caught up in the question of the extent to which Chaucer "augmented" English with French words (p. 72), a concern that I disclaim on the ground that Chaucer's contribution was to compose cultivated poetry in the Franglais already current in the royal court and inns of court.

45. Baugh and Cabel, *History* 177.

46. The difference between "stressers" and "timers" is considered by Paull F. Baum, *The Principles of English Versification* (Harvard, 1922) chap. 1. Baum discusses Chaucer prosody in *Chaucer's Verse* (Duke University Press, 1961).

47. Quoted from Helen Waddell, *Medieval Latin Lyrics* (1929; New York: Penguin, 1952) 266. Her verse translation reads: "O valley, still be gay, / Valley with roses climbing all the way, / Among all valleys valley one, / Valley the fairest in the hills."

48. Quoted from J. H. Fisher and D. Bornstein, *In Forme of Speche is Chaunge* (New York: Prentice, 1974) 130.

49. Susanne Woods, *Natural Emphasis: English Versification from Chaucer to Dryden* (San Marino, CA: Huntington Library, 1984) chap. 2.

2. Chaucer and the Inns of Court

1. Crow and Olson, *Chaucer Life Records,* chap. 3.

2. Crow and Olson, *Chaucer Life Records* 370.

3. On the importance of ransoms, May McKisack, *The Fourteenth Century* (Oxford: Clarendon, 1959) 246ff.

4. On Chaucer's silences, Paull F. Baum, *Chaucer: A Critical Appreciation* (Duke UP, 1958) 21–23.

5. Anatole de Montaiglon and Gaston Raynaud, *Recueil général et complet des fabliaux de XIII* et XIV* siècles,* 6 vols. (Paris: Libraire des bibliophiles, 1872–90). The best recent discussion in English is Charles Muscatine, *The Old French Fabliaux* (Yale UP, 1986).

6. Joseph Bédier, *Les Fabliaux,* 6th ed. (Paris: Champion, 1964).

7. See Per Nykrog, *Les Fabliaux* (Copenhagen: Munksgaard, 1957).

8. Henri Bergson, *Laughter,* trans. Brueton and Rothwell (New York:

Macmillan, 1911); J. H. Fisher, "City and Country in the Medieval Fabliaux," *Medieval Perspectives* (The Southeastern Medieval Association) 1 (1968): 1–15.

9. Speght, "Life of Chaucer" 22. Rickert, "Was Chaucer a Student at the Inner Temple?" 20–31; see Preface, note 1. The demurrals against the hypothesis that Chaucer studied in the inns are cited in the Preface.

10. Sir John Fortescue, *De Laudibus Legum Anglie,* ed. and trans. S. B. Chrimes (Cambridge UP, 1942).

11. On the origin and nature of the inns of chancery and of court, T. F. Tout, "The English Civil Service in the Fourteenth Century," *Bulletin of the John Rylands Library* 3 (1916): 185–214; "The Household of Chancery and its Disintegration," in *Essays Presented to R. L. Pool,* ed. H. W. C. Davis (Oxford: Clarendon, 1927); "Literature and Learning in the English Civil Service in the Fourteenth Century," *Speculum* 4 (1929): 365–89; *Chapters on Mediaeval Administrative History,* 6 vols. (Manchester UP, 1920–33) esp. vol. 1. J. H. Fisher, "Chancery and the Emergence of Standard English in the Fifteenth Century" 870–99.

12. On the inns of chancery as preparatory schools for the inns of court, William Holdsworth, *History of English Law,* vol. 12 (London: Methuen, 1903–12) 40ff.

13. George William Sanders, *Orders of the High Court of Chancery,* vol. 1 (London: A. Maxwell, 1845) 4; Tout, "Household of Chancery" 67.

14. Crow and Olson, *Chaucer Life Records* 148.

15. Philip Smith, *History of Education for the English Bar* (London: Butterworths, 1860) 10–11.

16. Chaucer's circle of associates is documented most thoroughly by Strohm, *Social Chaucer,* chaps. 1–3, but he organizes them by their affiliations to the court instead of by their civic activities. I am completely willing to accept the centrality of the court, but the point of this chapter is that Chaucer and the rest of London bureaucratic and merchant society had an existence that was independent of the court, and that most of Chaucer's writings can be more appropriately viewed as addressed to this civic audience.

17. Sylvia Thrupp, *The Merchant Class of Medieval London* (U of Michigan P, 1948) chap. 1. On the London population see also May McKisack, *The Fourteenth Century* 312ff.; Gervase Matthew, *The Court of Richard II* 64ff.

18. Jill Mann, *Chaucer and Medieval Estates Satire* (Cambridge U P, 1973) appendix A, gives lists of the order in which the estates appear in twenty-two representative pieces. Ecclesiastics head the lists in all but three: the twelfth-century *Livre des manières,* which begins with kings; the thirteenth-century *Chessbook,* which lists no ecclesiastics; and Chaucer's General Prologue.

19. The relationship between Chaucer and Gower is discussed by J. H. Fisher, *John Gower, Moral Philosopher and Friend of Chaucer* (New York UP, 1964) esp. chap. 5.

20. A. B. Emden, *A Biographical Register of the University of Oxford,* vol. 3 (Oxford: Clarendon, 1959) 1807.

21. R. W. Chambers and Marjorie Daunt, *A Book of London English: 1384–1425* (Oxford: Clarendon, 1967) 18ff., summarize the political imbroglio and print Usk's English "appeal" accusing Northampton and asking for clemency. Their notes cite biographical information about Usk in the London chronicles. W. W. Skeat, *The Works of Geoffrey Chaucer,* 7 vols. (Oxford: Clarendon, 1894–97;

hereafter *Oxford Chaucer*) gives a sketch of Usk's career and cites the borrowings from Chaucer in *Testament of Love* (7.xxiii).

22. Sylvia Thrupp, *The Merchant Class of Medieval London.*

23. H. G. Richardson, "Business Training in Medieval Oxford," *American Historical Review* 46 (1941): 259–80; "Letters of the Oxford *Dictatores,*" in *Formularies which Bear on the History of Oxford,* ed. H. E. Salter, W. A. Pantin, and H. G. Richardson, Oxford Historical Society, N.S. 4–5 (1942). R. J. Schoeck, "On Rhetoric in Fourteenth-Century Oxford," *Mediaeval Studies* 30 (1968): 214–15.

24. J. H. Fisher, "Chancery and Standard Modern Written English," *Journal of the Society of Archivists* 6 (1979): 143.

25. The "call to the bar" by which the student was converted into a barrister was a ceremony conducted within the inn. As described in the *Encyclopaedia Britannica,* 11th ed., s.v. "Inns of Court": "It takes place after dinner (before dinner at the Middle Temple which is the only inn at which students are called in their wigs and gowns), in the 'parliament', 'pension', or 'council chamber' of the benchers. The benchers sit at a table round which are ranged the students to be called. Each candidate being provided with a glass of wine, the treasurer or senior bencher addresses them and the senior student briefly replies. 'Call parties' are also generally held for the new barristers."

26. My information about the revels and literary connections of the inns is taken from A. Wigfall Green, *The Inns of Court and Early English Drama* (Yale UP, 1931) chap. 1.

27. The two ballades are short poems 14 and 18 in J. H. Fisher, *Complete Poetry and Prose.*

28. Although *Troylus* is dedicated to Gower and Strode, it is one of Chaucer's works that we know must have been in the library of Henry V. Morgan ms. 817 bears on the first page the arms of Henry when he was Prince of Wales. I shall in the last chapter associate this with the possibility that Henry promoted the copying of Chaucer's poems as models of cultivated English. Margaret Galway, "The 'Troilus' Frontispiece," *Modern Language Review* 44 (1949): 161–77, identified as members of the royal family the figures in the gorgeous frontispiece in Corpus Christi Cambridge ms. 61 of Chaucer reading *Troylus* to a richly garbed audience. But Derek Pearsall, "The *Troilus* Frontispiece and Chaucer's Audience," *Yearbook of English Studies* 7 (1977): 68–74, has argued cogently that the frontispiece was produced at the initiative of the manuscript's publisher, in the iconographic tradition of preachers standing in pulpits. The reciter has no book before him in the Corpus picture, and Pearsall prints three illustrations of preachers that are very similar indeed to the Corpus. Clearly the Corpus illustration was produced after Chaucer's death and tells us nothing about the original audience for the poem, although it might be further evidence of the royal promotion of Chaucer's works after 1400.

29. On the occasions of *Parliament of Fowls* and *House of Fame* see Haldeen Braddy, *Chaucer's Parliament of Fowls in Relation to Contemporary Events,* 2d ed. (New York: Octagon, 1969).

30. Larry D. Benson, "The Occasion of the *Parliament of Fowls,*" in *Wisdom of Poetry: Essays in Honor of Morton Bloomfield,* ed. Larry D. Benson (Kalamazoo, MI: Medieval Institute, 1982) 123–44, has argued that *PF* deals with negotiations for Anne of Bohemia, not Marie of France, but this would not affect the question of the audience for the poem.

31. Interpretation of *Troylus and Criseyde* as the first English novel began with J. J. Jusserand, *A Literary History of the English People* (New York, 1895), and G.L. Kittredge, *Chaucer and His Poetry* (Harvard UP, 1915). C. S. Lewis, "What Chaucer Really Did to *Il Filostrato*," *Essays and Studies* 17 (1932): 56–75, argues that Chaucer converted Boccaccio's novella into a romance.

32. The account of the meeting with the king is in Gower, *Works* 3.4–5. The similarities between the prologues of *Legend* and *Confessio*, and the possibility that the two pieces were commissioned at the same time by Richard and Anne are dealt with by J. H. Fisher, *John Gower* 235–43.

33. Deschamps's ballade is printed with translation in J. H. Fisher, *Complete Poetry and Prose* 952.

34. On sending *Legend* to Chaucer by the hand of Lewis Clifford, see J. L. Lowes, "The Prologue to the *Legend of Good Women* as Related to the French Marguerite Poems and the *Filostrato*," *PMLA* 19 (1904): 593–683.

35. On the political implications of the *Legend*, see J. H. Fisher, *John Gower* 243–47.

36. On the *ars dictaminis* and the formularies, see Murphy, *Rhetoric in the Middle Ages* 217 et passim.

37. E. J. Y. Bentley, "The Formulary of Thomas Hoccleve," diss., Emory University, 1965.

38. The Rivington syllabus quoted from Howard Brown, *Elizabethan School Days* (Oxford UP, 1933) 78.

39. R. W. Chambers, *On the Continuity of English Prose from Alfred to More and His School*, in Harpsfield's *Life of More*, EETS 186 (1932).

40. Norman Davis, "Styles in English Prose," in *Actes du 8ᵉ Congrès de la Fédération Internationale des Langues et Littératures Modernes* (Liège, 1961). These matters have been summarized by Ian A. Gordon, *The Movement of English Prose* (London: Longmans, 1966) chaps. 2 and 3.

41. Margaret Galway, "The 'Troilus' Frontispiece" 161–77.

42. North, *Chaucer's Universe* 38.

43. J. M. Manly, "Litel Lowis My Sone," *TLS* 7 June 1928: 430.

44. North, *Chaucer's Universe* 7; 169ff. are devoted to the authorship of the *Equatorie*, which North accepts as a Chaucer holograph.

45. Paul Strohm, *Social Chaucer*, chaps. 1–3.

3. Chaucer and the Emergence of the Individual

1. For a comprehensive introduction to the medieval view of society see Walter Ullman, *The Individual and Society in the Middle Ages* (Johns Hopkins UP, 1966).

2. Speght's "Life of Chaucer," in Hammond, *A Bibliographical Manual* 24ff.; Thynne, *Animadversions*.

3. On mimology, see Gerard Gennette, *Mimologiques: Voyage en Cratylie* (Paris: Seuil, 1976), discussed and chap. 12 translated by Thäis E. Morgan, *PMLA* 104 (1989): 202–14.

4. All citations to Chaucer allusions before 1900 are to the chronological

listing in C. F. E. Spurgeon, *Five Hundred Years of Chaucer Criticism and Allusion, 1357–1900* (1908–17; NY: Russell, 1960). Dryden in Spurgeon 1.278; Blake in Spurgeon 2.43.

5. On the effect of improved education on the perception of the individual, see Colin Morris, *The Discovery of the Individual, 1050–1400* (1972; U of Toronto P, 1987) chaps. 2 and 3.

6. I owe a good deal of the following discussion of the emergence of the sense of authorship among scholastic teachers to A. J. Minnis, *Medieval Theory of Authorship: Scholastic Literary Attitudes in the Later Middle Ages* (London: Scholar, 1984).

7. On Hugh of St. Cher, R. H. and M. A. Rouse, "The Verbal Concordance of the Scriptures," *Archivum Fratrum Praedicatorum* 44 (1974): 5–30. On Robert and Henry Stephens, *Religious Encyclopaedia,* ed. Philip Schaff, vol. 3 (New York: Funk, 1890) 274.

8. Minnis, *Medieval Theory of Authorship,* chap. 1.

9. Minnis, *Medieval Theory of Authorship,* chap. 4.

10. John Wyclif, *De veritate sacrae Scripturae,* as discussed by Minnis, *Medieval Theory of Authorship* 143–44.

11. Beryl Smalley, *English Friars and Antiquity in the Early Fourteenth Century* (Oxford: Blackwell, 1960).

12. Leo Spitzer, "Note on the Poetic and Empirical 'I' in Medieval Authors," *Traditio* 4 (1946): 414–22.

13. Walter Ong, "The Author's Audience is Always Fiction," *PMLA* 90 (1975): 9–21.

14. Morris Bishop, trans., *Letters from Petrarch* (Indiana UP, 1966) 5.

15. Kevin Brownlee, *Poetic Identity in Guillaume de Machaut* (U of Wisconsin P, 1984).

16. Sara Jane Williams, "An Author's Role in Fourteenth-Century Book Production: Guillaume de Machaut's 'Livre ou je met toutes mes choses,'" *Romania* 90 (1969): 433–54.

17. Gower, *Complete Works* 3.446–67.

18. A. C. Outler, ed. and trans., *Augustine's Confessions,* vol 7 (Philadelphia: Library of Christian Classics, 1955) 6.3.

19. On *lectio* in the Benedictine Rule, Adalbert de Vögué, *The Rule of Saint Benedict: A Doctrinal and Spiritual Commentary,* trans. J. B. Hasbrouck (Kalamazoo, MI: Cistercian Publications, 1983): 242–47. On Cluniac adaptations, L. J. Daly, *Benedictine Monasticism* (New York: Sheed and Ward, 1956) 156.

20. J. H. Fisher, "Chaucer and Written Language," in *Popular Literature of Medieval England,* ed. T. J. Heffernan (U of Tennessee P, 1985).

21. Paul Saenger, "Silent Reading: Its Impact on Late Medieval Script and Society," *Viator* 13 (1982): 367–414.

22. The figures accompanying the *Astrolabe* and *Equatorie* are reproduced in J. H. Fisher, *Complete Poetry and Prose.*

23. "To Adam Scryven," short poem 15 in J. H. Fisher, *Complete Poetry and Prose.*

24. On Deschamps's ballade and Usk's borrowing from Chaucer, see the discussion in chap. 2 above.

25. Chaucer, *Treatise on the Astrolabe*, in J. H. Fisher, *Complete Poetry and Prose* 908–37.

26. Erich Auerbach, *Mimesis: The Representation of Reality in Western Literature*, trans. Willard Trask (Princeton UP, 1953).

27. On the penitential tradition, C. R. Cheney, *English Synodalia in the Thirteenth Century* (Oxford UP, 1941); "Penance and Penitentials," in *Dictionary of the Middle Ages*, vol. 9 (New York: Scribners, 1987) 487, has a good bibliography.

28. See Theodor von Karjan, ed., "Sermones nulli parcentes," *Zeitschrift für Deutsches Althertum* 2 (1842): 6–92.

29. Ruth Mohl, *The Three Estates in Medieval and Renaissance Literature* (Columbia UP, 1933). On the difference between generalized complaint and particularized satire, John Peter, *Complaint and Satire in Early English Literature* (Folcroft, PA: Folcroft, 1956).

30. The point of view of J. M. Manly, *Some New Light on Chaucer* (1926; New York: Peter Smith, 1952) is extended by Muriel Bowden, *A Commentary on the General Prologue to the Canterbury Tales*, 2d ed. (New York: Macmillan, 1967). Jill Mann, *Chaucer and Medieval Estates Satire* 203–6, gives the order of the estates in twenty-two listings.

31. John T. McNeil and Helena Gamer, *Medieval Handbooks of Penance* (Columbia UP, 1938) 414.

32. E. H. Gombrich, *Art and Illusion*, 4th ed. (London: Phaidon, 1972) 173.

33. On the physiognomic, exegetic, and astrological treatises, W. C. Curry, *Chaucer and the Medieval Sciences*, 2d ed. (New York: Barnes, 1962).

34. Earle Birney, "Is Chaucer's Irony a Modern Discovery?" in *Essays on Chaucerian Irony*, ed. Beryl Rowland (U of Toronto P, 1985) 37. Birney credits some of his observations to Edward F. Piper, "The Miniatures of the Ellesmere Chaucer," *Philological Quarterly* 3 (1924): 241–46.

35. Roger Ascham, in Spurgeon 1.91.

36. Morris, *The Discovery of the Individual* 73–75, 153–55, et passim.

37. W.F. Bryan and Germaine Dempster, eds., *Sources and Analogues of Chaucer's Canterbury Tales* (U of Chicago P, 1941).

38. Morris, *Discovery of the Individual* 70–75, 131–32, et passim.

39. On the background of the debate genre, H. Walther, *Das Streitgedicht in der lateinischen Literatur des Mittelalters*, Quellen und Untersuchungen zur lateinischen Philologie des Mittelalters, teil 1, bis 2 (Munich: Beck, 1914).

40. David Riesman, Nathan Glazer, and Reuel Denney, *The Lonely Crowd* (New York: Doubleday, 1955).

4. The Chaucerian Voice

1. Chaucer, *Treatise on the Astrolabe*, in J. H. Fisher, *Complete Poetry and Prose* 909.60.

2. Peter N. Heydon, "Chaucer and the *Sir Orfeo* Prologue of the Auchinleck MS," *Proceedings of the Michigan Academy of Science, Arts, and Letters* 51 (1966):

529–45; N. F. Blake, "Chaucer and the Alliterative Romances," *Chaucer Review* 3 (1969): 163–69; Elizabeth D. Kirk, "Chaucer and His English Contemporaries," in *Geoffrey Chaucer, A Collection of Original Essays,* ed. George Economu (New York: McGraw, 1975).

3. H. G. Pfander, "Some Medieval Manuals of Religious Instruction in England and Observations on Chaucer's Parson's Tale," *JEGP* 35 (1936): 243–58; Siegfried Wenzel, "Chaucer and the Language of Contemporary Preaching," *Studies in Philology* 73 (1976): 138–61.

4. Derek Brewer, "The Relationship of Chaucer to the English and European Traditions," in *Chaucer and Chaucerians,* ed. Derek Brewer (U of Alabama P, 1966); Ian Robinson, *Chaucer and the English Tradition* (Cambridge UP, 1972); Alexander Weiss, *Chaucer's Native Heritage* (Berne: Lange, 1985).

5. Skeat, *Oxford Chaucer* 2.xxi-iv. T. W. Machan, "Editorial Method and Medieval Translation: The Example of Chaucer's *Boece,*" *Studies in Bibliography* 41 (1988): 188–96, finds the *Boece* translation much better than Skeat does: the awkwardness grows out of an effort at clarity and precision—but this still makes it "translation prose."

6. John Keats, letter to John Taylor, in *Selected Poems and Letters* ed. Douglas Bush (Boston: Houghton, 1959) 267.

7. On Chaucer's oral performance, a recent discussion with good bibliography is Beryl Rowland, "*Pronuntatio* and its Effect on Chaucer's Audience," *Studies in the Age of Chaucer* 4 (1982): 33–52.

8. The history of the Puis is found in H. T. Riley, ed., *Memorials of London Life in the 13th, 14th, and 15th Centuries* (London: Longmans, 1863). The regulations of the London Pui are in H. T. Riley, ed., *Monumenta Gildhallae Londoniensis: Liber Custumarum,* Rolls Series, 2 (1860), Pt. 1, 216; trans. Pt. 2, 579. Possible connection of Gower with the London Pui is discussed by J. H. Fisher, *John Gower* 78ff.

9. On Chaucer's prosody in general, Baum, *Chaucer's Verse*; his indebtedness to the English tradition, Ian Robinson, *Chaucer's Prosody: A Study of the Middle English Verse Tradition* (Cambridge UP, 1971). See also Dorothy Everett, "Chaucer's Good Ear," *Review of English Studies* 23 (1947): 201–08; Percy Adams, "Chaucer's Assonance," *JEGP* 71 (1972): 527–39. Bibliographical citations to twenty-eight recent studies of Chaucer's prosody (nos. 112–30) are listed in Mark Allen and J. H. Fisher, *The Essential Chaucer: An Annotated Bibliography of Major Modern Studies* (Boston: G. K. Hall, 1987).

10. Nicholls, *The Matter of Courtesy*; Boase, *Origin and Meaning of Courtly Love*; Kendrick, *The Game of Love*; Green, *Poets and Princepleasers,* chap. 4

11. Andreas Cappelanus, *The Art of Courtly Love,* trans. J. J. Parry (Columbia U P, 1941).

12. The psychological interpretation was initiated by Bertrand H. Bronson, "The *Book of the Duchess* Re-opened," *PMLA* 67 (1952): 863–81.

13. G. L. Kittredge, "Chaucer and Some of His Friends," *Modern Philology* 1 (1903): 1–18. J. L. Lowes, "The Prologue to the *Legend of Good Women* as Related to the French Marguerite Poems and the *Filostrato*" 593–683, and "The Prologue to the *Legend of Good Women* Considered in Its Chronological Relations," *PMLA* 20 (1905): 749–864. James I. Wimsatt, *The Marguerite Poems of Guillaume de Machaut,* University of North Carolina Studies in Romance

Languages and Literatures, no. 87 (1970). A summary and bibliography on the relations of the *Legend* to the *marguerite* poems is in J. H. Fisher, "The *Legend of Good Women*," in *Companion to Chaucer Studies,* ed. Beryl Rowland, 2d ed. (New York: Oxford, 1979).

14. Wimsatt, *Chaucer and the French Love Poets* 93–94.

15. Elaine T. Hansen, "Irony and the Antifeminist Narrator in Chaucer's *Legend of Good Women*," *JEGP* 82 (1983): 11–31.

16. Wayne C. Booth, *The Rhetoric of Fiction* (U of Chicago P, 1961) chap. 1.

17. Green, *Poets and Princepleasers,* chap. 5.

18. Galway, "The 'Troilus' Frontispiece."

19. Chaucer's development from the style of Guillaume de Lorris to that of Jean de Meun is the subject of Charles Muscatine, *Chaucer and the French Tradition* (U of California P, 1957).

20. Murphy, *Rhetoric in the Middle Ages* 220–22, 233–34, et passim.

21. B. J. Whiting, *Chaucer's Use of Proverbs* (Harvard UP, 1922). Donald MacDonald, "Proverbs, *Sententiae,* and *Exempla* in Chaucer's Comic Tales: The Function of Comic Misapplication," *Speculum* 41 (1966): 453–65.

22. Murphy, *Rhetoric in the Middle Ages* 232.

23. Robert J. Allen, "A Recurring Motif in Chaucer's *House of Fame*," *JEGP* 55 (1956): 393–405; Alfred David, "A Literary Satire in the *House of Fame*," *PMLA* 75 (1960): 333–39.

24. Dieter Mehl, "The Audience of Chaucer's *Troilus and Criseyde*," in *Chaucer and Middle English Studies in Honour of Rossell Hope Robbins,* ed. Beryl Rowland (London: Unwin, 1974); "Chaucer's Audience," *Leeds Studies in English* 10 (1978): 58–74.

25. Laurence Sterne, *The Life and Opinions of Tristram Shandy, Gentleman,* ed. J. A. Work (New York: Odyssey, 1940) 103.

26. Jane Austen, *Mansfield Park* (London: Dent, 1934) 411.

27. Discussion of the nature of the persona of Chaucer the pilgrim was introduced by E. T. Donaldson, "Chaucer the Pilgrim," *PMLA,* 69 (1954): 928–36. There are nine items on this topic cited in Allen and Fisher, *The Essential Chaucer,* nos. 70–86.

28. Booth, *Rhetoric of Fiction* 158–59.

29. G. L. Kittredge, *Chaucer and His Poetry* 73. Bronson, "*Book of the Duchess* Re-opened."

30. General discussion of irony is in Norman Knox, *The Word Irony and Its Context, 1500–1755* (Duke UP, 1961). Chaucer's irony is explored by Earle Birney, *Essays on Chaucerian Irony.*

31. St. Augustine, *De Doctrina Christiana* 1.37.23, *Patralogia Latina* 34.81. Quoted from Rowland in Birney, *Essays on Chaucerian Irony* xvi.

32. John Peter, *Complaint and Satire in Early English Literature* (1965; Folcroft, PA: Folcroft, 1969).

33. Recent neo-historical critics maintain that Gower and Langland, as well as medieval critics of society like Bernard of Cluny (*De contemptu mundi*) and Henry of Huntington (*Satira communis*), are satirists because they say they are, and that John Peter's distinction between satire and complaint is anachronistic. But this does not address the difference between the playful, specific Chaucerian voice and the somber, generalized Gowerian voice, between hortatory and

entertaining, between sentence and solas. See Paul Miller, "John Gower, Satiric Poet," in *Gower's Confessio Amantis, Responses and Reassessments,* ed. A. J. Minnis (Cambridge: Brewer, 1983); J. H. Fisher, *John Gower* 206–7.

34. John Burrow, *Ricardian Poetry: Chaucer, Gower, Langland, and the Gawain Poet* (Yale UP, 1971) chap. 3.

35. David Riesman, Nathan Glazer, Reuel Denny, *The Lonely Crowd,* and see above, the end of chap. 3.

36. David Benson, *Chaucer's Drama of Style: Poetic Variety and Contrast in the Canterbury Tales* (U of North Carolina P, 1986) makes contrast the principle of organization in the Canterbury collection.

37. I shared an office with Mr. Ransom one summer at USC, and this wonderful line, like the one on the last page of this book about recognizing genuine poetry by the hairs rising on the back of the neck, came from our memorable conversations.

38. John Henry Newman, *Apologia pro vita sua* (Oxford UP, 1964) chap. 1.

39. Newman, *Apologia* 2.

40. J. R. R. Tolkien, "Chaucer the Philologist," *Transactions of the Philological Society,* 1934, 1–70.

41. Denis de Rougemont, *Love in the Western World,* trans. Montgomery Belgion, rev. ed. (New York: Pantheon, 1956).

42. Robert Worth Frank, *Chaucer and the Legend of Good Women* (Harvard UP, 1972).

43. John Fyler, *Chaucer and Ovid* (Yale UP, 1979).

44. Roger Sherman Loomis, "Was Chaucer a Free Thinker?" in *Studies in Medieval Literature in Honor of Albert Croll Baugh,* ed. MacEdward Leach (U of Pennsylvania P, 1961).

45. Fyler, *Chaucer and Ovid* 22.

5. Chaucer since 1400

1. R. K. Root, "Publication before Printing," *PMLA* 28 (1913): 417–31; A. I. Doyle and M. B. Parkes, "The Production of Copies of the *Canterbury Tales* and *Confessio Amantis* in the Early Fifteenth Century," in *Medieval Scribes, Manuscripts and Libraries: Essays Presented to N. R. Ker,* ed. M. B. Parkes and A. G. Watson (London: Scholar, 1978).

2. W. Carew Hazlitt, *The Livery Companies of the City of London: Their Origin, Character, Development and Social and Political Importance* (1892; New York: Blom, 1969), Scriveners Guild, 613ff.; Stationers Guild, 629ff.. The Scriveners Guild was evidently the original. Its members were designated "Writers of Court-hand and text-letters." In the fifteenth century, stationers were book sellers, in contrast to scriveners who were public stenographers. Stationers were first mentioned in 1379 when "stations" were granted to eleven women in St. Paul's Churchyard for the purpose of selling small wares. In 1403 the London Corporation acceeded to an ordinance "of writers of text-letter, limners, and others who bind and sell books." Limners were the scribes who executed the floriated initials and borders.

3. N. F. Blake, *Caxton's Own Prose* (London: Deutsch, 1973) 100.

4. Marshall McLuhan, *The Guttenberg Galaxy* (U of Toronto P, 1962) chap. 124.

5. A. S. G. Edwards and Derek Pearsall, "The Manuscripts of the Major English Poetic Texts," in *Book Production and Publishing in Britain, 1375–1475,* ed. A. S. G. Edwards and Derek Pearsall (Cambridge UP, 1989) 257–78, estimate that there are extant about thirty secular manuscripts in English from before 1400 and six hundred from after 1400.

6. Margaret Deanesley, *The Lollard Bible* (1920; Cambridge UP, 1966) vii, "The mere possession of English books, and especially English scriptures, might make a man suspect of heresy."

7. J. H. Fisher, *John Gower,* chap. 3 and appendix A.

8. J. H. Fisher, "*Piers Plowman* and Chancery Tradition," in *Medieval Studies Presented to George Kane,* ed. E. D. Kennedy, R. Waldron, J. S. Whittig (Cambridge: Brewer, 1988). David Fowler in a private communication disagrees with this count (based on the manuscript descriptions in the Kane-Donaldson edition) and proposes that some ten *Piers* manuscripts date from before 1400, but this would still be ten out of sixty.

9. J. H. Fisher, "Animadversions on the Text of Chaucer," 779–93.

10. E. F. Jacob, *The Fifteenth Century, 1399–1485* (Oxford: Clarendon, 1961) esp. chap. 3; B. Wilkinson, *Constitutional History of England in the Fifteenth Century* (1964; New York: Barnes, n.d.)

11. G. L. Harriss, *Henry V* (Oxford UP, 1985) chap. 1, "The Exemplar of Kingship," describes the national devotion that Henry evoked. Fisher, Richardson, and Fisher, *An Anthology of Chancery English,* print all of Henry's English signet letters.

12. J. H. Fisher, *John Gower* 116–34.

13. G. L. Harriss, *Cardinal Beaufort* (Oxford: Clarendon, 1988) chap. 1.

14. Recent historians doubt the Oxford tradition (see Harold F. Hutchinson, *Henry V: A Biography* [New York: John Day, 1967] 18), but the fifteenth-century chronicle evidence is cited by *DNB,* s.v. "Henry V" and "John Rous." On Beaufort as tutor to Henry V, Harriss, *Cardinal Beaufort* 9; *DNB,* s.v. "Henry Beaufort." On the movements of Beaufort and Prince Henry 1398–1403, Harris, *Cardinal Beaufort,* chap. 1.

15. Derek Pearsall, *John Lydgate* (UP of Virginia, 1970) 29. Pearsall discusses in detail Chaucer's influence on Lydgate, which he interprets as purely artistic, whereas I interpret it as partly political—the result of Henry V's promotion of cultivated writing in English. This political sponsorship would also help to account for Lydgate's own reputation and influence, which Pearsall details.

16. N. F. Blake, *The Textual Tradition of the Canterbury Tales* (London: Arnold, 1985) chaps. 4–9.

17. J. M. Manly and Edith Rickert, eds., *The Text of the Canterbury Tales,* vol. 1 (U of Chicago, 1940) 159.

18. Aage Brusendorff, *The Chaucer Tradition* (Oxford: Clarendon, 1925) 186.

19. John Norton-Smith, *John Lydgate: Poems* (Oxford: Clarendon, 1966) 195; Pearsall, *John Lydgate* 30–31.

20. John Lydgate, *Troy Book,* ed. Henry Bergen, EETS, ES, 97 (1906).

21. Walter F. Schirmer, *John Lydgate,* trans. Ann E. Keep (London: Methuen, 1952) 41.

22. Thomas Hoccleve, *Regement of Princes,* ed. F. J. Furnivall, EETS, ES, 72 (1897).

23. Jerome Mitchell, *Thomas Hoccleve* (U of Illinois P, 1968) 110–14.

24. Henry Scogan, "Moral Balade," in Skeat, *Oxford Chaucer* 7.xli and 237–44.

25. Spurgeon 1.14–20ff.

26. N. F. Blake, *Caxton's Own Prose* 61–62. The brief prologue to *Confessio Amantis* is on 69–70.

27. Sir Philip Sidney in Spurgeon 1.121.

28. Ben Jonson in Spurgeon 1.193.

29. Thomas Morrell in Spurgeon 1.381–82.

30. William Alderson and A. C. Henderson, *Chaucer and Augustan Scholarship* (U of California P, 1970).

31. Eleanor N. Adams, *Old English Scholarship in England from 1566–1800,* Yale Studies in English, no. 55 (New Haven: 1917).

32. Penn R. Szittya, *The Antifraternal Tradition in Medieval Literature* (Princeton UP, 1986).

33. *Statutes of the Realm,* vol. 3 (1817), 1963, 34–35 Henry VIII, chap. 1.

34. John Foxe in Spurgeon 1.105–06.

35. "Jack Upland" is printed in Skeat, *Oxford Chaucer,* vol. 7. The Cowden-Clarke ascription is cited in Spurgeon, 3.194.

36. Thomas Usk in Spurgeon 1.8; Lydgate in Spurgeon 1.13 et passim, discussed above; Hoccleve in Spurgeon 1.21, discussed above; Sir Brian Tuke in Spurgeon 1.79–80.

37. Ballade from Deschamps, J. H. Fisher, *Complete Poetry and Prose* 952, second stanza, first line.

38. Gower, *Confessio Amantis* 8.2940–50.

39. Sir Philip Sidney in Spurgeon 1.122.

40. E. Talbot Donaldson, *The Swan at the Well: Shakespeare Reading Chaucer* (Yale UP, 1985).

41. Chaucer had been "adapted" as early as 1520. One-third of *Fair Custance,* printed by Richard Pynson, is a modernization of the Man of Law's Tale. See Franklin B. Williams, Jr., "Alsop's *Fair Custance*: Chaucer in Tudor Dress," *English Literary Renaissance* 6 (1976): 351–68.

42. Daniel Javitch, *Poetry and Courtliness in Renaissance England* (Princeton UP, 1978); Frank Whigham, *Ambition and Privilege: The Social Tropes of Elizabethan Courtesy Theory* (U of Colorado P, 1984).

43. Harington in Spurgeon 1.134; R. K. Root, *The Poetry of Chaucer* (Boston: Houghton, 1922) 176; Derek Brewer, "The Fabliaux," in *Companion to Chaucer Studies,* ed. Beryl Rowland, 296.

44. Ruth Kelso, *The Doctrine of the English Gentleman in the Sixteenth Century* (1929; New York: Peter Smith, 1964); *The Doctrine of the Lady in the Renaissance* (U of Illinois P, 1956).

45. Ascham in Spurgeon 1.85; Foxe in Spurgeon 1.105; Scott in Spurgeon 1.124; Letter in Spurgeon 1.224.

46. William Webbe in Spurgeon 1.129.

47. Erich Auerbach, *Mimesis: The Representation of Reality in Western Literature,* trans. Willard Trask (Princeton UP, 1953)

48. All of the citations to Dryden's *Fables* are to Spurgeon 1.272–84.

49. John Dryden, "To the Reader," *The Hind and the Panther*, in *The Poetical Works of John Dryden*, ed. G. R. Noyes (Boston: Houghton, 1909) 218.

50. Leigh Hunt in Spurgeon 2.269.

51. Matthew Arnold in Spurgeon 3.129.

52. Manly's edition of *The Canterbury Tales* omits or bowdlerizes the Miller's, Reeve's, and Cook's Tales, the Wife of Bath's prologue, and the Physician's, Shipman's, and Manciple's Tales, as well as compressing the Monk's Tale, Melibee, and the Parson's Tale.

53. Auerbach, *Mimesis* 9.

54. Anatole de Montaiglon and Gaston Raynaud, *Recueil général et complet des fabliaux des XIIIᵉ et XIVᵉ siècle*; Joseph Bédier, *Les Fabliaux*.

55. Thomas Ross, *Chaucer's Bawdy* (New York: Dutton, 1972); Jean-Charles Huchet, *L'amour discourtois: La "Fin amors" chez les premiers troubadours* (Toulouse: Privat, 1987); Kendrick, *The Game of Love*; Nykrog, *Les Fabliaux*.

56. C. S. Lewis, *The Allegory of Love* (1936; New York: Oxford U P Galaxy, 1958) 176.

57. D. W. Robertson, Jr., and Bernard Huppé, *Piers Plowman and Scriptural Tradition* (Princeton UP, 1954); D. W. Robertson, Jr., *A Preface to Chaucer* (Princeton UP, 1962).

58. Usk in Spurgeon 1.8.

59. Robert E. Kaske, *Medieval Christian Literary Imagery: A Guide to Interpretation* (U of Toronto P, 1989).

60. W.R. Crawford, *Bibliography of Chaucer, 1954–63* (U of Washington P, 1967) xx–xxiii, gives a good introduction, with citations, to the rediscovery since 1951 of "complexity" in Chaucer's poetry.

61. Foxe in Spurgeon 1.106; Lodge in Spurgeon 1.117; Webbe in Spurgeon 1.129.

62. Paul Olson, *The Canterbury Tales and the Good Society* (Princeton UP, 1986); Julia Bolton Halloway, *The Pilgrim and the Book: A Study of Dante, Langland, and Chaucer* (Berne: Lange, 1987); Charles Dahlberg, *The Literature of Unlikeness* (UP of New England, 1988).

63. Terry Jones, *Chaucer's Knight: The Portrait of a Medieval Mercenary* (Louisiana State UP, 1980).

64. Judson Boyce Allen, "The Old Way and the Parson's Way: An Ironic Reading of the Parson's Tale," *Journal of Medieval and Renaissance Studies* 3 (1973): 255–71.

65. Elaine Hansen, "Irony and the Antifeminist Narrator in Chaucer's *Legend of Good Women*."

Index

For a list of abbreviations, see page 173.

John H. Fisher is editor of *The Complete Poetry and Prose of Geoffrey Chaucer*, 2d ed. (New York: Holt, 1989) and author of *John Gower, Moral Philosopher and Friend of Chaucer* (New York UP, 1964) and many other books and articles. He has taught at several universities, the longest at New York University and most recently at the University of Tennessee, Knoxville. For eight years he served as executive secretary of the Modern Language Association and as editor of *PMLA*. In 1979 he cofounded the New Chaucer Society and served for eight years as its director.